A Voice from Africa

God bless you.

[signature]
05-19-21

A Voice from Africa

Tales of a Radio Broadcaster

Isac Silvano

Some names and identifying details have been changed to protect the privacy of individuals.

The author has tried to recreate events, locations, and conversations from his memories of them. In some instances, in order to maintain their anonymity, the author has changed the names of individuals and places. He may also have changed some identifying characteristics and details such as physical attributes, occupations, and places of residence.

Copyright © 2021 by Isac Silvano

All rights reserved. No part of this book may be reproduced or transmitted in any form or by any means, electronic or mechanical, including photocopying, recording, or any information storage and retrieval system, without permission in writing from the author.

ISBN: 978-1-6653-0139-8 - Paperback
eISBN: 978-1-6653-0140-4 - ePub
eISBN: 978-1-6653-0141-1 - mobi

Printed in the United States of America   033021

∞This paper meets the requirements of ANSI/NISO Z39.48-1992 (Permanence of Paper)

Scripture: New American Standard Bible
Cover Art: Josiane Zanon Moreschi

Scripture quotations marked "BSB" are from The Holy Bible, Berean Study Bible, copyright © 2016 by Bible Hub. Used by Permission. All rights reserved worldwide.

Scripture quotations marked "NKJV" are taken from the New King James Version®. Copyright © 1982 by Thomas Nelson. Used by permission. All rights reserved.

Scripture quotations marked "KJV" are taken from the Holy Bible, King James Version (Public Domain).

Stories in Introduction taken from testimonies received through the years.

I dedicate this book:

To my wife, Helena, your companionship and faithfulness throughout the years have been invaluable; during good and challenging times in our lives as a couple and as missionaries. We have made beautiful memories, which in turn have enriched the content of this biography.

To my daughters, Djamila and Priscila. Thank you for understanding the call on my life to preach the gospel. Together we have experienced the blessings and challenges of serving the Lord in the mission field and beyond.

To Peter Widmer and Martin Voegelin, your friendship and counsel have meant the world to me. Thank you for believing in me and challenging me to write this book, and giving all the support I needed to make this a reality.

Silvano Family in Swaziland-1996

Foreword

As a young mission leader, I was put in touch with an Angolan pastor and missionary I did not know. I wanted to meet him in São Paulo and find out how his already-running Radio Ministry to Angola could be developed. Radio Trans Mundial do Brasil, Trans World Radio in Swaziland, an IESA church in Angola, and the Swiss Mission should be the partners involved. It sounded rather complicated, but the encounter with Isac, and, very soon, also Helena, was just very special to me. Their commitment and availability were inspiring, and our conviction to go for this adventure with many risks and promising fruit was growing. With the support from experienced people, it was confirmed step by step: God had prepared the way.

Nevertheless, the many people, organizations, circumstances were putting the Silvanos often to the test: Love it or leave it! I thank God He strengthened Helena and Isac again and again—cared from various sides for them even when we as a mission were not aware of the real issues behind. I thank you, Isac, you *never* complained, you kept the vision clear and fought for it in a special, gentle way! It's more than thirty years now, and what started as a shy getting-to-know-each-other has grown into a deep, meaningful friendship in which we still discover the richness God has laid into our respective lives!

I'm also thankful Isac is telling us here and there how battles (from in- and outside) were painful processes. The way he overcame, how he did not lose heart—all was equipping him to be the messenger of the Good News he is up to now! He is convinced there is always a lesson to learn, a chance to grow. Because of his work, many people suffering from war, injustice, hatred, lack of home, or basic supply in Angola were encouraged, comforted, and led to reconciliation with people and with God!

Walking with Christ is an ongoing journey of growth. High peaks and deep valleys make part of it. This book is more than just a biography, more than about Radio Ministry, it's about how God changed and is changing life! It's about a caring, personal God. Take advantage from the lessons Isac is sharing!

Martin Voegelin
Winterthur, Switzerland, June 30, 2020

***

I met Isac Silvano several years ago when he began attending a Wednesday morning men's worship meeting that I was a part of. I was immediately drawn to him. Very quickly it became obvious to me that this was a special man who was full of the love of Christ. Here was a man that was truly humble before the Lord, grateful to be able to serve in Christ's Kingdom, thankful for the grace and goodness of God in his life, and so encouraging to his brothers and sisters in Christ. Here was a man of passionate prayer and time-tested trust in the faithfulness of God.

Isac and Helena's story is a testimony of the plan and providence of God in the lives of those who trust in Him. It is a story of the unfolding of God's calling in the lives of those who diligently seek Him. It is the story of God's faithfulness through life's challenges and disappointments.

This book is packed with a lifetime of Godly wisdom and life lessons learned on the mission field by a family who committed their lives to walk humbly before their God and to serve Jesus their King, going wherever He has called them to go, and doing whatever He has asked them to do with diligence, cheerfulness, and gratitude, giving all the glory to God! May we all be inspired by their living example.

David Nutter
Atlanta, Georgia
September 20, 2020

Preface

Time is a funny thing. We fight with it and tell it to speed up in our adolescence, only to turn around and yell at it to slow down in our golden years. We rejoice when it brings with it wisdom, maturity, and experience but despise it when it robs us of agility, memories, and opportunities. Even though time has a funny way of giving while taking, one thing that it has given me is the ability to look back and see the big picture of the amazing plans that God had for my life, and how involved He has been in every intricate detail.

Isac recording at the national radio station in Angola

Introduction

He woke up and knew, without looking at the clock, what time it was. Years of routine had given his body an internal clock that went off every morning at four. Being careful not to wake his wife, he slipped out of bed and made his way to the walk-in closet that he had set up as a home studio. He began to pray, asking the Lord to guide and direct him in the day's activities. After some time of Bible reading and meditation, he turned on his computer and pulled up the scripts that he finished working on the night before. Years of experience taught him that his voice was at its best early in the morning. He switched on all the recording equipment, put on his headphones, positioned his scripts, drew close to the microphone, and pressed record. *"Alô amigo ouvinte. Aqui estamos novamente conectados através das ondas de rádio . . ."*

"Alô amigo ouvinte. Aqui estamos novamente conectados através das ondas de rádio . . ." came the familiar voice through the radio. Although it was early, the whole family gathered together to listen. As head of the house, he felt responsible for his family's spiritual growth and made a point of gathering them together on mornings like this. The fact that he had an early shift at the hospital didn't stop him from making time for this program; he had learned so much from these teachings and appreciated how they dealt with issues they faced there in Angola. He glanced at his family members' attentive faces, each one taking in the topic for that day's message.

"Alô amigo ouvinte. Aqui estamos novamente conectados através das ondas de rádio . . ." She looked forward to tuning in and hearing these messages every week. Not just because she learned so much from the teachings, but because they had radically changed her life. She thought back with regret at the years she had lived without Christ and how empty her life had been. Since she started listening to the programs, she had joined a church there in Mozambique and found happiness she didn't know was possible. She drew her attention back to the words that were coming from the radio and listened carefully. After all, these words were helping her build good character, and to her, that was a priority.

"Alô amigo ouvinte. Aqui estamos novamente conectados através das ondas de rádio . . ." Church had started, but in this case, it was being held in the living room of their home. As a farmer living in the country with no churches nearby, he and his family were far from the city life that Brazil had to offer. He looked at the radio, a gift left by those who had brought the Gospel to his home, and smiled. This radio station and these programs had become their church, carrying them through the most difficult time in their lives. Gratitude didn't even begin to describe how he felt when they sat together and listened to a life changing Word like this.

How does God take one man and use him to impact the lives of people around the world?

Part 1
The Early Years in Angola

Isac with his parents-1991

My Childhood Home

I was born in the small village of Ebanga, in the province of Benguela, Angola on October 4, 1947. We were nine children in total: five boys and four girls. Our house was always full, if not with guests that my parents liked to entertain then with cousins that would come and stay with us for extended periods of time. I remember times when there were seventeen people living in our house.

Our house had four bedrooms, a living room, and dining room with the kitchen and bathroom separate from the rest of the house. My parent's room was the only one with a bed because having beds in our rooms took up much needed space. At night, we would sleep on mats on the floor underneath our own individual blankets. When we got up in the morning, we would roll up our mats and put them away.

We lived off the land and raised cattle. Waking up at four in the morning to go to the fields, till the land, and plant different kinds of crops was a normal part of our morning routine. At 7:00 a.m., we would go back home, get ready for school and eat our breakfast, which usually consisted of a sweet potato, roasted corn on the cob, or porridge. We would then walk to school.

I look back and wonder how seventeen people could live in a four-bedroom house, or how we could work and go to school at such a young age. Needless to say, this type of lifestyle was very difficult for us as children, but time has given me an appreciation for how it formed me. I thank God, and my parents, for teaching me the value of hard work and preparing me for life.

Even after leaving my parent's house to go to high school in the city of Lubango, which was about 350 kilometers away, I never gave up my routine of working in the fields. During our two-month break from school, I would go back home and help my parents reap the wheat harvest manually. To thresh the wheat, we would first lay it out on a concrete pad until it dried. Then with a yoke of oxen, we would go over the wheat several times, and as the oxen would tread on it, we would remove the outer casing. Next came the gathering of the wheat. Using a sift, we would throw it up in the air and the wind would blow away the chaff, leaving the wheat to fall on the canvas on the ground. I cannot say how many times I performed this task, but years later, it would help to bring another level of understanding when I read scriptures in the Bible, where Jesus uses agricultural symbolism to describe Kingdom principles. From the proceeds of our wheat sales, my father would give me some money to take back with me for school expenses.

As a young man, I learned to work hard and discovered that work gives a person dignity. When I would share with my schoolmates what I had done during my break, they were always amazed and had a certain level of respect for me, to the point of asking me for advice when they were faced with problems.

> *"If you are willing and obedient, you will eat the best of the land."*
> —Isaiah 1:19

My Parents Find Christ

Shortly after I was born, my father found out that a missionary from the Swiss Alliance Mission, known at that time as "Mission Filafricana," or Friends of Africa, had an intriguing black-covered book that made one wise. My father decided to walk to the mission compound, which was about thirty kilometers away, to talk to the missionary, look at the book, and, if possible, buy it. His plans to buy it were unnecessary because the missionary showed him the book and, to his surprise, gave him a copy that was in his own native language. She also shared the gospel with him, and he accepted Christ as his Savior that very day. Later, the missionary invited him to move with our family to the missionary station in our village.

While helping my father grow in his new faith, the missionary would take the opportunity to share the gospel with my mother. After some time, she also accepted Christ as her Savior. A few months later, my father went to the mission station in Kalukembe to study theology at their Bible Institute. After completing a two-year course, he returned to Ebanga as an evangelist and was later consecrated to the pastoral ministry. It amazes me to see how God timed everything perfectly to ensure that I grew up in a Christian home.

> *"You did not choose Me but I chose you, and appointed you that you would go and bear fruit, and that your fruit would remain, so that whatever you ask of the Father in My name He may give to you."*
> —John 15:16

My Dreams and Desires

Ever since I could remember, my dream was to be a professional race car driver. Since we didn't have the financial means to make that happen, I decided to use a bicycle as a way of racing. As a teenager in the early 1960s, I was able to save enough money to buy a bike by selling sugar cane that grew on our farm. I started racing against my friends, and even some adults, right there in Ebanga and soon became known as one of the best in the area. Our competitions were purely for bragging rights as the winner never received anything because there was no money to buy prizes. My love of racing only grew with time, and later, I bought a motorcycle. I encouraged my fellow competitors to do the same so we could race, but they weren't able to save enough money to buy the motorcycles for cash. Back then, financing anything wasn't an option, let alone a dream. I became frustrated that I couldn't live out my dreams of racing cars, or even motorcycles.

My other dream was to become a doctor. This too didn't pan out because there were no universities in Angola back then. The only way to study medicine was to go to a university in Portugal, but my parents didn't have the finances to cover the cost of the trip, or tuition for six years of medical school. This too was another frustrating reality for me, but in time, I discovered that God had another wonderful plan for my life.

> *"For I know the plans I have for you, declares the LORD, plans to prosper you and not to harm you, to give you a future and a hope."*
> —Jeremiah 29:11 (BSB)

How I Found Christ

The fact that I grew up in a Christian home didn't mean I automatically earned the right to become a Christian. I was in church every Sunday, was baptized, and even sang in the youth choir; but Jesus was not my Savior. I was religious and did everything habitually and mechanically, but a true relationship with Christ was something foreign to me. What I needed was my own personal encounter and experience with Jesus Christ and the Father.

In 1961, Angola began its quest for independence from the nation that had claimed it as its colony, Portugal. As a result, the Portuguese government arrested and imprisoned several Angolans, whom they considered to be sympathetic to the independence movement, that were fighting against the Portuguese army from bases they had set up in neighboring countries. Many that were arrested died in jail. My uncle, who became a pastor at the same time as my father, suffered this fate. In his case, however, he was arrested simply for preaching the gospel. The authorities claimed that his messages would open people's minds to a different political reality.

The day my father found out about my uncle's death, he called a family meeting. I remember it like it was yesterday: all nine of us looking at my father and wondering what could possibly be the cause for this meeting, and his dejected demeanor.

"My children," he said, "You know that our nation is at war. Your uncle who is in jail has been killed, and who knows if the same will not happen to any one of us tomorrow. I called this family meeting to give you this sad news. I also want to say that from this day forward, your mother and

I are no longer responsible for your lives before God because we have shared with you the gospel and shown you the way to salvation. In this time of uncertainty and fear in our nation, I fear for anyone who does not have Jesus Christ as his Lord and personal Savior because without Christ, you are completely lost and condemned to hell."

Hearing these words felt like being pierced by a double-edged sword. I left the meeting and ran like a madman toward the forest, crying. I started yelling, "I want Jesus! I want Jesus! I want Jesus!" By then, I was deep in the forest, had stopped running, and was no longer crying. I felt a peace that cannot be described in words, and it was at that exact moment that Jesus heard my cry, forgave my sins, and came into my heart.

Someone might say, "Okay, but if you were going to church and singing in the choir, how was life different for you after this experience?" The truth is that even though I was only fifteen at the time, I started to see the world through the lens of what Jesus Christ and the Father meant to me. I felt compassion for those who were living in sin and had not experienced salvation. It wasn't hard for me to stop practicing the wrong things that had grieved my parents and God. I did this not by my own willpower but by the strength that came from God to have victory over temptation and sin. Suddenly, I had this strong desire to tell others about Jesus but had no knowledge of how to do it nor the courage. I told my father that I wanted to be just like him and preach the gospel. Time has helped me realize that God not only saved me then but also set me apart to proclaim the gospel. However, this would only become a reality twelve years later. The Bible says that our ways are not God's ways. God may delay, but He never fails to fulfil His promises.

"But when God, who had set me apart even from my mother's womb and called me through His grace, was pleased to reveal His Son in me so that I might preach Him among the Gentiles . . ."
—Galatians 1:15-16

My Early Academic and Professional Life

Military service- Army, Infantry Sergeant

I did part of my elementary education at the Evangelical missionary school in Ebanga. After some time, and for reasons beyond my understanding, my father had me transferred to a public elementary school that was seven kilometers from the mission station. In 1963, I moved to the city of Lubango to attend high school. Although the sons and daughters of other pastors were given the opportunity to live in the house that the church had in Lubango, for some reason I was not given that opportunity. Instead, my older brother found a small room that was an extension to a house where I lived alone for the next five years while in high school. My family sacrificed a lot to provide the finances for my education, but I studied hard, made good grades, and graduated.

At the age of twenty-one, I was called to serve in the Portuguese army. It was during this time that the movements for "liberation from colonial rule," based in the neighboring countries, were fighting against the army for Angola's independence. I trained at the Sergeant's school in the city of Huambo and after graduating, I was transferred to the city of Lubango. For two years, I served in the infantry's recruitment and immobilization department. My responsibilities included overseeing the uniforms in the supply room and distributing them to the new recruits.

As I was carrying out my duties, I found out that there was a Portuguese officer who was not my immediate superior, who wanted a copy of the key to the supply room. A fellow Sergeant friend of mine got wind of it and warned me not to give the official a key because if anything went missing, I was the one who would be held responsible and officially charged by my superior. I later found out that it was not uncommon for those who previously held my position to sell part of the uniform and keep the money. This is exactly what the Portuguese official was planning on doing. So, when I refused to give him the key, he was furious, but didn't say a word to me. His lack of response surprised me and I thought that after being met with resistance, that maybe he had given up on his illegal scheme. Little did I know that he was looking for an opportune time when I would be alone in the supply room, catch me unaware, and beat me. Now this was a strong man who was an avid boxer before he joined the army. If he was a heavyweight, then I was a lightweight; I would have been knocked out before the fight even began. So ridiculous were my chances, a friend of this official warned me when he found out about his plan.

I knew I needed help in protecting myself but wasn't sure what to do. So, I did the only thing I could and would kneel and pray every morning for God's protection before heading off to work. I would also pray that I would be transferred to another military base. Once at work, I would maintain this attitude of prayer, especially when I was in the supply room. As I was handing out uniforms one day, the Portuguese official started coming at me like a lion ready to pounce, but when he entered the supply room, his mood changed drastically, and he started talking to me in a normal way. This happened on three occasions, but the Holy Spirit would intervene and disarm him every time. I started to understand a little how David felt when he had to deal with King Saul and his fits of murderous rage. Through it all, I never gave up my prayer vigils and after a few months, I received my orders of a transfer to the city of Huambo.

On the day of my departure, I got a surprising summons to the Portuguese official's office. As soon as I went in, he closed the door, which filled my heart with trepidation. I thought for sure this was the end of my life and my military career. He stood on the other side of his desk, looking at me, and said, "Sergeant, I tried several times to knock you out for not giving me the key to the supply room. But every time I tried, I would lose strength as soon as I walked in the room and my arms would almost feel paralyzed. I had no clue what would come over me or what was happening to me. Your honesty and dedication to your job and your friendly demeanor to the recruits has really impressed me. Please don't take my ill will and failed plans against you to heart. Have a good trip and all the best in your military career."

I was shocked and stood there speechless. It wasn't so much what he said, because I knew what had been going on and how the Lord was protecting me, but the fact that I never would have expected this level of humility from him in admitting it. Although he never apologized for his behavior, his attitude was more powerful to me than hearing the words "I'm sorry." I thanked him and wished him God's best. Although my time at that military base was difficult, and an unpleasant way to start my military career, it taught me very early on the faithfulness of God and the incredible power of prayer.

Shortly after arriving at my new post in Huambo, I was promoted and later sent to the front lines in the eastern part of Angola. Six months later, I was wounded in combat during an attack by the opposition. Eight soldiers died that day, but my life was spared. Time has allowed me to look back and realize how God preserved me for His greater plan.

Wounded, I was quickly taken to the military hospital in the capital city of Luanda and rushed to the operating room, so they could remove a bullet that was lodged near one of my vertebrae. The surgery was successful, but they had to graft and join two vertebrae that were damaged. The recovery process took nine months, six of which I was on complete bed rest and on my back. The extended recovery was due to a decision the doctor made not to put me in a cast because he feared the high temperatures the city was experiencing would provide a breeding ground for wounds to form under the cast. Power outages were a frequent occurrence, and there were days when the infirmary would go hours without power and air conditioning.

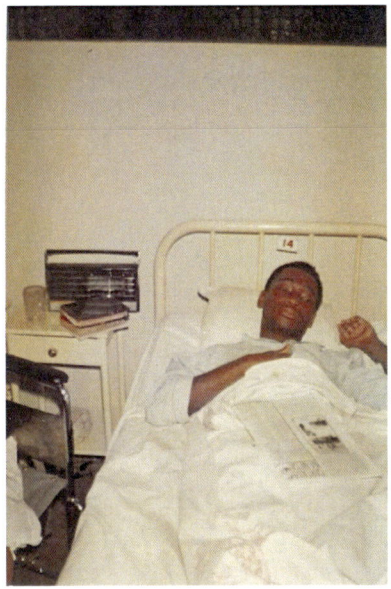

Military hospital, recovering from surgery

Seven months after the surgery, and just as I celebrated my twenty-seventh birthday, I started trying to walk again by holding on to the walls, like a child trying to take its first steps. Two months later, I was discharged from the hospital and medically discharged from the army. All was not in vain though, as these months in the hospital brought about a wonderful encounter that could only have been ordained by God.

"Do not fear, for I have redeemed you; I have called

you by name; you are Mine! When you pass through the waters, I will be with you; and through the rivers, they will not overflow you. When you walk through the fire, you will not be scorched, nor will the flame burn you. For I am the LORD your God, the Holy One of Israel, your Savior . . ."

—Isaiah 43:1-3

My First Engagement

During the year I served in the army in the city of Huambo, I had a girlfriend who later became my fiancée. Back then, an engagement was something very serious, not only for the couple, but for their families as well. Although we were not intimate, our engagement had the same weight as a marriage, one which could not be terminated without the consent of both families.

A few months before my deployment to the frontlines, I discovered a character trait in my fiancée that she had hidden from me. I prayed about it and came to the conclusion that it would not be wise to continue the relationship. I was conflicted because I had to look in my fiancée's eyes and tell her that it was over, but first, I had to announce to both families my decision to end our engagement.

Before I spoke to her, I sought advice from my aunt, who told me to tell my fiancée as soon as possible. My aunt also offered to go with me when I went to tell our families. It may seem strange that I went to seek counsel from my aunt and not one of my uncles, but I wanted to get a single woman's perspective, and find out how she might feel and react if this had happened to her.

The conversation with my fiancée was not easy, but my aunt had advised me to be frank with her, so, with determination and conviction, I told her that we had to end our engagement. I said that we could continue as friends, but nothing more. It was a moment of sadness and tears, but it was best to sever ties rather than end up in a situation we would both regret later.

As promised, my aunt was by my side when I went to break the news to our families. Thankfully, we were able to end the engagement without any problems or ill will between us, or between our two families. My aunt's help was vital because in our culture, aunts and uncles were respected and held an important role of mentors and protectors of their nieces and nephews. In the absence of parents, they would take on the responsibility of educating and providing for the children financially as well as giving them moral and spiritual guidance. They were essentially a second set of parents.

This relationship and subsequent engagement were my first. Needless to say, I was a little apprehensive after it didn't work out, so I prayed and told the Lord that I would not date until He showed me, without a shadow of a doubt, the woman that I should marry. Four years later, God sent me a woman who was beautiful inside and out and was always happy regardless of the circumstances around her.

> *"Truthful lips will be established forever . . ."*
> —Proverbs 12:19

Meeting Helena

God brought Helena to me during special circumstances. During the nine-month recovery process after my back surgery, I stayed in the hospital wing that held army sergeants and officials. I was in a room that had six beds and one day, they brought in another sergeant who was recovering from surgery on his left shoulder. They put him in the bed across from mine and we became friends. Little did I know that he was Helena's uncle.

The first time that Helena came to visit her uncle and our eyes met, it was as if time stood still. Her uncle introduced us, and I was thrilled by how friendly she was and impressed by the joy that radiated from her. I thought to myself, *what a beautiful woman, if only I could marry someone like that.* I figured there was no way she would even look at me, considering the state that I was in. The truth is that God ignited a flame in both of our hearts on that very first encounter.

Every time Helena would visit her uncle, she would come over to my bed and we would talk. Time passed, and a friendship was formed. The friendship grew, to the point where her visits continued long after her uncle was discharged from the hospital. She wouldn't come empty-handed either and always brought a little something, like delicious cakes that she had baked. After many visits and several cakes later, we started dating.

When the doctor told me that I could start leaving the hospital on weekends, Helena's uncle invited me to come and stay at her parents' house where he was staying. I had no family in Luanda, so his invitation turned out to be not only convenient but enjoyable. Helena's parents and nine siblings were a happy family, and I felt at home with them. I would return to the hospital on Mondays and wait for the medical committee's decision on whether I would be able to continue my service in the army. I waited for about a month before finding out that my army days were over for good.

With my life no longer in the hands of the army, I asked Helena to marry me and she gladly accepted. With the help of her uncle, I went to her parents and asked for their blessing, and they gave it to me without objection. Then, accompanied by her older brother and sister, Helena and I traveled to my village in the south so I could introduce her to my family. Both my parents and my siblings loved her, and the engagement process was now complete.

"An excellent wife, who can find? For her worth is far above jewels." —Proverbs 31:10

The Call to Pastoral Ministry

Meeting Helena was not the only significant thing that happened during my nine-month recovery period in the hospital. I also received the call to become a pastor and teach the word of God.

Even before my official medical discharge from the army, it became clear to me that I wasn't going to continue with my military career because of the extent of my injuries. So, I would pray a lot and ask God to reveal what His purpose and will was for my life. On the morning of August 2, 1974, I was lying in bed and reading Psalms 50, when I came across verse 15 which says: "Call upon Me in the day of trouble; I will deliver you, and you shall glorify Me." I thought about how God had protected me during combat and how He used the doctor to remove the bullet that was lodged near my spinal cord. I got emotional and while expressing my gratitude to God, the Holy Spirit reminded me of what I said to my father years ago: "I want to be just like you and preach the gospel." I knew without a doubt that God wanted me to glorify Him by becoming a missionary and preacher of the gospel. I told the Lord that I was ready to do His will. So when I started dating Helena, I told her right away that I was going to study theology and become a pastor.

God used my time in the hospital to not only call me but prepare me for ministry. Time has given me perspective and helped me realize that this was the best time of my life in terms of communion with God and the strengthening of my faith.

My faith was tested several times in that hospital. The enemy used other sergeants to try to discourage me and distance myself from God. There was a Portuguese sergeant that was being treated in the hospital wing that I was in. He was discharged but three months later was readmitted with injuries caused by fragments from a grenade. When he found me laying on the same bed, reading my Bible, he said, "Isac, what evil did you commit against God to suffer like this? This can only be punishment from a God who has completely abandoned you, and you're still reading that black book you call a Bible! If I were you, I would never again speak of this God of yours that is cruel and unjust." I told him not to worry about me because God was not responsible for my suffering. That I was suffering, like many others, because of the senseless war in our country. I went on to tell him that God was in complete control of my life.

While others saw my condition and time in the hospital as suffering, for me, it was a great opportunity to grow spiritually and receive many blessings from God. It was during my hospital stay that I met my wife, was called by God to become a pastor, received a scholarship to study theology in Rio de Janeiro, Brazil, and was introduced to a man who later paid for my ticket to go to Brazil. Who would have thought that a military hospital could turn out to be such a blessing?

> *"And we know that God causes all things to work together for good to those who love God, to those who are called according to His purpose."*
> —Romans 8:28

Move to Brazil

Two days before I was discharged from the hospital, the military committee met to evaluate my health and recovery from the surgery. They concluded that although I was healthy, I was physically unable to continue my service in the army, and I was medically discharged in November of 1974.

Just before my discharge, I received a letter from the First Baptist Church in São Paulo, Brazil, offering to pay for my studies at the seminary in Rio de Janeiro. However, I had to pay for the ticket to get there. The church also informed me that the students would start school at the end of February 1975. I was elated and disappointed at the same time because I didn't have enough funds for the ticket and all the other expenses that go along with an international trip, like paying for a passport and visa applications. I talked to my parents to see if they could help with the expenses and as much as they wanted to, it was simply out of the question. I was confused, a bit angry at God because the things He had told me while on my hospital bed were not lining up with the latest developments. Questions ran through my mind about the trustworthiness of the Word of God and His ability to fulfill His promises.

I resigned myself to the fact that I wasn't going to Brazil and decided to look for a job instead. I asked acquaintances if they knew of any openings and if they could help me in any way. The job search was very difficult because the Portuguese government was in the process of giving Angola, and other African colonies, their independence. It didn't matter what door I knocked on with my resumé, nothing opened up.

The second Sunday in January of 1975, I visited the Third Baptist Church of Luanda. A few people knew me there and one of them, a gentleman who had visited me in the hospital, welcomed me and called me up front to introduce me to the church. He asked me to give a testimony about my time in the hospital and talk about my plans for the future. I told them about how God had spared my life during combat, and how my back surgery had saved me from possibly being paralyzed from the waist down. I also shared about my call to become a pastor, the scholarship I had received to study theology in Brazil, and the fact that I had no way of getting there because I had to pay for the ticket to Rio de Janeiro. I concluded by asking them to pray for me, and they did so right then and there.

At the end of service, the gentleman that had introduced me told me to start packing because he was going to pay for my ticket to Rio de Janeiro. I found out later that he was Danish and the director of the shipping company "Cecil Brasil." He told me that I would be traveling on a ship that was leaving in thirty days.

I was overjoyed and anxious at the same time because there wasn't much time to get everything ready. I had to take Helena home to meet my parents and at the same time say goodbye to my family. I also had to get a Portuguese passport and sell a few things so I wouldn't travel penniless. I didn't waste any time. I left the church that day and immediately started on my to-do list. In three weeks, I was ready for the trip.

I boarded the "Cecil Brasil," the cargo ship bound for Rio de Janeiro at the harbor in the city of Lobito, on February 25, 1975. The ship was well equipped with cabins that were mainly for the sailors but with two that were for passengers. Our nonstop trip took two weeks, and I was terribly seasick for the first two days, but the captain kindly provided some medicine that helped me the remainder of the way. As we made headway, the captain offered to send a telegraph to Helena to let her know that the trip was going well. I was grateful and happy when I found out that she received it.

Like their captain, the sailors were also very kind and attentive. They would come by my cabin to chat and make sure that everything was okay. We were given three meals and snacks throughout the day. The food was mainly seafood and delicious. I gained three kilos in fourteen days! Never had I eaten on land, food as delicious as what I savored on the high seas.

We arrived at the harbor in Rio de Janeiro at six in the morning on March 11, 1975. The ship stopped a distance away and waited for a spot to dock. The captain called the mainland to find out if there was someone there awaiting my arrival. There wasn't. He told me that since there was nobody waiting for me, the best thing would be to leave my suitcase on the ship, find out where the seminary was located, and then come back for my belongings. I agreed. I wouldn't have known what to do anyway since this was my first time on a ship, and outside of Angola, so everything was new to me.

A small boat came and took us to the main gate. I presented my passport and the immigration officer asked the reason for my visit, where I was staying, and how long I was going to be in Brazil. I gave him my invitation letter which had the seminary's address, told him that I was there to study theology, and that I had no idea how long I would be staying. He stamped my passport and with a friendly smile said, "Young man from Angola, welcome to Rio."

As I left the harbor, the first thing I saw was a busy street with cars and many people going to-and-fro. I got scared because I didn't know which way to go. Should I cross the street or go left or maybe right? I stopped and leaned on a pole and asked God to show me what to do. As I looked up and saw people walking and speaking in Portuguese, albeit with a slightly different accent, the fear dissipated.

I noticed a newspaper stand a few meters away and walked over to speak to the owner. He was a tall black man who appeared to be about my father's age. I explained to him my situation and where I was trying to go. He told me that he didn't know the street I was looking for, but the neighborhood was far away and I would need to take a taxi or a bus.

Since we used a different word for bus in Angola and I didn't know what he was referring to, I told him that I preferred to go by taxi. He asked me if I had enough money because it was going to be expensive. I told him that I had a few dollars with me. He then replied that I would need to go by the bank first and exchange them because the driver wouldn't accept dollars. He said, "My son, be very careful, you're in Rio de Janeiro! Don't tell anybody that you have dollars, or you and your dollars will disappear."

He pulled something out of his pocket and extended his hand to me saying, "Here, take this and go by bus." I asked him what that word that he kept saying meant. "You don't know what a bus is? It's the city's public transportation."

"Oh, I see. You're talking about the bus services," I replied. "Yeah, that's right, but that's the name for it in your country," he said. I then asked him where I should go and take the bus, but I used a Portuguese word that is normally used when referring to taking medicine. He said, "Here, we don't take the bus because it's way too big and would never fit in our mouths, much less down our throats. You can get the bus over there and tell the driver that you need to get off in Tijuca. When you get there, ask somebody for directions to the seminary." I thanked him and did just that and got off at the bus stop on a street called Bomfim, which was about a twenty-minute walk to the seminary. I obviously had a lot to learn about Brazil and was thankful for the kindness and good humor of this stranger God put in my path.

When I arrived at the seminary, the dean gave me a hearty welcome and took me to see the principal, who immediately asked his secretary to register me for classes. Then, the dean took me to every classroom and introduced me to the first and all the way to the fourth-year students. At that time, I was the first student to come all the way from Angola to do the four-year program so, my arrival was something new and exciting. There had been another young man from Angola, but he had studied theology in Portugal and came to the seminary just for a six-month internship before returning home.

That afternoon, I was able to exchange some dollars right there at the seminary, and while talking to some of the students, I mentioned that I had to go back to the harbor and pick up my suitcase. A third-year student walked over to me, gave me a hug, and said that he would go with me. It was already late, so I suggested we take a taxi.

When we arrived at the harbor, the ship had docked and was being unloaded. We went inside and I thanked the captain and said my farewells to the sailors. When we got to the main gate to exit the harbor, an officer stopped us and said that we needed to have the suitcase inspected by customs before we could leave. I tried to explain to him everything that happened earlier, how I had to leave my suitcase behind and was now coming back for it, but he had made up his mind and would not be moved. The student who had accompanied me tried to reason with him by saying that I was a Christian who had come to study theology at the seminary that he was also attending, and that there was nothing in my suitcase that was banned from entering the country. He was still not moved and insisted on opening the suitcase to check its contents.

Now this was a big suitcase that weighed more than thirty kilograms and was packed full of everything that I thought I could possibly need, including a portable typewriter. It was so full that I had to sit on it to close it, but not before I had placed a white handkerchief on top of my clothes and a Bible on top of the handkerchief. When the officer unlocked the suitcase, it burst open and the Bible flew out. "See," the other student said to him, "I told you he came to study at the seminary and there was nothing in the suitcase that would compromise his stay here." The officer paused, looked at me, told me to close the suitcase and that we were free to go. I sat on my suitcase and closed it.

What happened next shocked me and had a profound and lasting effect on me. My companion picked up the heavy suitcase, placed it on his head, and started walking out the gate. Still carrying my suitcase on his head, we walked to the area where we could get a taxi. I looked at him and was touched by his humble attitude and the brotherly Christian love he was showing me.

It was hard for me to believe that a white man was carrying a black man's suitcase, whom he had known for only a few hours. What was being displayed in front of me was far from the reality I was used to in Angola, where black people were servants and whites, masters. Never would a white man have carried a black man's suitcase, let alone carry it on his head. Hard and strenuous work was always left for black people.

We got in the taxi and I thanked him for his kindness. He said it was the least he could do. "I'm happy and grateful that God brought you here to study, so you can become an ambassador for Him in Angola." When we arrived at the seminary, he carried my suitcase from the taxi and up the stairs of our dormitory. Once in my room, he put the suitcase on the bed and said, "Welcome. Now we are friends. If you need anything, don't hesitate to come and find me." We prayed together, and he left. After he left, I knelt by the bed with tears of gratitude and thanked God for everything He had done for me and for the love shown to me by my new friend and brother in Christ. Later, my two roommates arrived and made me feel welcomed and right at home.

I stayed in that dormitory for only six months because that August, Helena arrived from Angola; and in September of 1975, we were married and moved to the building that housed married students.

> *"There is neither Jew nor Greek, there is neither slave nor free man, there is neither male nor female; for you are all one in Christ Jesus."*
> —Galatians 3:28

Part 2
Birth of a Ministry in Brazil

Our Wedding

Before I left Angola, I told Helena and her parents that upon completing my first year at seminary, I would return so we could have the wedding ceremony and then take her back with me to Brazil. At that time, Angola was still under Portuguese jurisdiction, but the winds of independence were already sweeping through the country. Anticipating the coming storm and the uncertainty that it would bring, I suggested that Helena start the process of getting a Portuguese passport, so that if she needed to leave the country she could do so without any problems. I was also thinking ahead to my return in December, making sure we wouldn't have the added stress of applying for her passport. We could simply have the ceremony and then travel to Rio de Janeiro.

After I arrived in Brazil, Angola began its pursuit for independence and later achieved it on November 11, 1975. Although the quest for independence promised new freedom, it also brought political unrest due to disagreements between the different parties in the independent movement. I watched with great apprehension as the situation unfolded, realizing that if I returned to Angola as planned in September, they would not let me leave, as the government had placed restrictions on young people leaving the country. I had no idea what would become of our wedding plans and became overwhelmed with fear, to the point of despair. There were nights when I couldn't sleep and my studies began to suffer. To add to that, there was the very difficult conversation I eventually had with Helena and her parents, letting them know of my decision not to return to Angola.

All this uncertainty and anxiety was taking its toll on me,

so I set out to try to find a solution. Since I had a Portuguese passport, I decided to go to their embassy and talk to the consul. He was very welcoming and listened as I explained my dilemma. When I asked for his recommendations, he looked at me and said, "Are you really serious about marrying this woman because an engagement can be terminated and you could easily find someone else here in Brazil?" I told him that Helena was a gift that God had given me and that I was not interested in marrying anyone else, Brazilian or otherwise. I went on to tell him that if he could help me, I was ready to cover whatever the costs were for the process.

Surprised by my conviction and seeing the determination in my eyes, he said, "The only option is for the embassy to prepare a document that would allow your fiancée to have a civil ceremony in Angola and for someone to stand in for you and sign on your behalf. With that done, and the marriage certificate in hand, she could then leave Angola and join you here." The consul had no idea how those words had just lifted an enormous burden that had been my companion for days. I could finally breathe again and did so, taking a deep breath as I smiled at the prospect of seeing a light at the end of a very dark tunnel.

That same day, the consul prepared the documents and the following day, I sent them to Helena after having explained everything to her. She had agreed to, in essence, get married without me. I was relieved when her brother agreed to stand in for me but my joy was short-lived when I found out her father's thoughts on the matter. Her father sent me a message letting me know in no uncertain terms that if I wanted to marry his daughter, I would have to go to Angola. The message went on to say that he had no intentions of letting her go through with the wedding by herself, let alone travel unaccompanied to Rio de Janeiro.

Prayer was the only option that Helena and I had to deal with her father's decision, so we dedicated ourselves to it, seeking Divine guidance. We prayed that if our plans to get married in this manner were indeed God's will, then her father would have a change of heart, without any influence or pressure from other family members. It didn't take long for our prayers to be answered. A few days later, Helena's father gave us his blessing, and the ceremony proceeded as planned. For Helena and I, this was confirmation that we were indeed in God's will, and it was of great encouragement to us.

When I met Helena, she was working as an assistant in the accounting department at the Coffee Institute of Angola. After we got engaged, she faithfully started saving money every month to buy things for her trousseau-clothes, household linen for her marriage, which she kept in a big suitcase. After months of saving and shopping, Helena was rewarded by the sight of a bulging suitcase, and we decided to send it ahead of her, a few weeks before her departure. I suggested that she have it delivered to the director of the Cecil Brasil ships, who would send it to Rio de Janeiro on one of their vessels. This turned out to be a huge mistake.

The suitcase was indeed delivered to the director, but mysteriously disappeared at the harbor. It was incredibly difficult for us to come to terms with this, especially Helena. I still remember hearing the anguish in her voice when she asked me, "Why did you suggest I send the suitcase on that ship? My father could have sent it by plane! Now what am I going to do?" What do you say to a bride who has dreamed and saved for a trousseau for months, and it disappears into thin air in a matter of hours?

I tried to console her as best I could and then sent a

letter to the ship's director demanding that he do something to find that suitcase. He replied, "Isac, I did everything in my power to try to find this suitcase, but they threatened to kill me if I continued to investigate its disappearance. It is no longer safe here, especially for foreigners. A lot of us have already left, including most of the Portuguese. My wife and I are still here but we don't know for how long. You left at the right time and I am so glad you did. Now, the young people here can no longer travel abroad and they have stopped issuing visas and passports. They are forcing them to join the army because the new government is anticipating some serious fighting against the other two parties in the independence movement." And with that, our hopes of ever seeing Helena's precious trousseau disappeared. The only thing she had left was her wedding dress, which thankfully she had decided to set aside and take as carry-on luggage.

When everything was ready for Helena to embark on her journey to Rio de Janeiro, I communicated her arrival date to the pastor at the First Baptist Church in São Paulo. The church graciously asked a family that lived in the south side of Rio if Helena could stay with them until the day of our wedding, this time the religious ceremony. I also shared with my classmates and the director of the seminary the day that Helena was scheduled to arrive. A friend who owned a car told me not to worry about transportation because he would go with me to the airport.

When we arrived at the airport, we stood at a strategic spot where we could see the passengers as they entered a huge room to get their luggage. I was so anxious that my heart raced with anticipation every time a passenger entered that room. I was also worried about what would happen to me if for some reason she didn't arrive. Back then, communication was not quick and easy like it is today and there were no cell phones, instant messages, or e-mails. Since she was taking a long time to come out, my anxiety started increasing with each passing moment and my friend noticed. He put his arm around my shoulder and said, "Isac, be patient. She'll be out soon. Everything will be okay." As soon as he said that, there was Helena, looking beautiful and walking into the big room to pick up her luggage. I breathed a sigh of relief and yelled, "She's here!" A woman who was standing near us, asked who "she" was. I said, "My fiancée."

"Congratulations," she said, "I hope you two will be very happy."

We dropped Helena off in Copacabana, at the home where she would stay while arrangements for our wedding were being made by the church in São Paulo. I was unable to visit Helena regularly during her stay there as my classes and preparations for the wedding left me little time to go and see her. Trying to find a suit within my limited budget was trickier than I expected, so I spent a good deal of time going from one store to another. At one point during my search, a deacon at the church in São Paulo, who happened to be a tailor, called and gave me the wonderful news that he wanted to make my suit as a wedding present. He told me to go and see a tailor friend of his there in Rio, who would take my measurements and send them to him. I did so that same day.

A few weeks later, the church finalized all the arrangements and Helena and I traveled to São Paulo. Upon our arrival, the church surprised us by announcing that our wedding would be at the Baptist church in the city of Campos de Jordão, which happened to be one of the most beautiful cities in the state. The city sits up in the mountains and is known as the "Switzerland of Brazil" due to similarities in architecture and breathtaking views. With this as our backdrop, we were married on September 27, 1975, and stayed on for our honeymoon.

> *"Be anxious for nothing, but in everything by prayer and supplication with thanksgiving let your requests be made known to God. And the peace of God, which surpasses all comprehension, will guard your hearts and your minds in Christ Jesus."*
> —Philippians 4:6-7

Our Time at Seminary

After our honeymoon, we returned to the seminary in Rio de Janeiro, where we stayed in the building that housed the married students who had no children. The building had big rooms and communal bathrooms, one for the ladies and another for the men. For the rooms, the seminary provided a bed, table and chairs, and a sofa. Each couple was left to arrange their room as they liked. I had started getting some things together and arranging the room before Helena and I left for our wedding.

I purchased a bright red stove and refrigerator because it happened to be in one of my favorite colors. I am color-blind and have always liked bright colors so, when I saw these appliances, I was sold. I also bought cooking utensils, silverware, and dishes. I then bought a curtain, which I used to close off the area where the bed was to give it more privacy. With the remaining space, I created a section for the kitchen and dining room.

The famous red stove

    We returned from our honeymoon and I led Helena to the room that would be our new home. She commended me on what I had done, and in time, went on to rearrange just a few things that were more to her liking. There was, however, something that didn't strike her fancy but she didn't mention it. It wasn't until years later that I found out that she never liked that red stove and refrigerator. She was wise not to say anything back then because there was no way that I could have returned them since they were bought on credit and the store wouldn't have let me exchange them. Besides, we didn't have the means to buy another pair in the color of her liking. Helena had to put up with that red refrigerator and stove for years because fortunately, or from her perspective unfortunately, they were very well made and lasted a long time. They made it through several moves to different cities in Brazil, and the only reason we finally got rid of them was because we moved to a place where they couldn't go. But more on that later.

Apart from that, we were very happy in our room/home. I remember when the lady that Helena stayed with in Copacabana came to visit, she walked in and said, "What a beautiful room. Everything is in its place, and your stove is so clean. It's like you've never even used it!" I am so grateful that as a couple, Helena and I have always shared the same values of taking good care of our home and keeping it tidy.

At the beginning of 1976, Helena enrolled in classes for a degree in music. That September, our first daughter was born. At that time, we had classes in the mornings and didn't have anyone to stay with our child. There was no way we could afford a babysitter. We prayed and asked God to show us what to do, and He answered our prayers in a very special way. Our daughter developed a sleeping pattern where she would stay awake most of the night and sleep all through the morning. So, while we were in classes, we asked our neighbor, who never left her room in the mornings, to regularly check on her as she slept. Since our building was very close to where I had classes, I also talked to my teachers about letting me leave class for a few minutes every day so I could check and make sure that everything was ok. This was our routine until we moved to the building that had apartments for couples with children. Our apartment was on the second floor and had a living room, kitchen, and one bedroom. We were able to leave our daughter with one of our neighbors in the building and eventually, a young lady came to live with us and helped take care of her.

Both my theology and Helena's music degrees took four years to complete, but I was a year ahead of her. So, when I graduated and we moved to São Paulo to serve as missionaries of the First Baptist church there, Helena had to finish her studies at the Baptist Theological College of São Paulo. As Helena was completing her final year, I was ordained a minister in February of 1979. My first missionary assignment from the church was to plant a new Baptist church in a small town called Mococa.

First year at seminary as a married couple

While still living in São Paulo, I would travel to Mococa alone every weekend to do evangelism and start the new church. The salary we received as missionaries from the church was not enough to support our family. So, to supplement our income, I worked Monday through Friday nights at a call center for the counseling department of the American Evangelist Rex Humbard's television ministry.

Time has helped me realize how these counseling sessions over the phone expanded my knowledge of the Bible because for every call, which required me to listen more than talk, I had to read a Bible verse to the caller before praying with them. Although the nights were tough and my shifts long, from 5:00 to 11:00 p.m., they bore lasting fruit. On more than one occasion, I had people come to my office and tell me the transformation that God had done in their lives through one of those phone calls.

Meanwhile, Helena completed her course and graduated with her music degree in December of 1979. The following month, our second daughter was born and shortly after that, we were invited by the church to move to Mococa so I could become the pastor to a forty-three-member congregation.

> *"For who has despised the day of small things?"*
> —Zechariah 4:10

At the seminary with fellow classmates. Isac is pictured front row, first on the right

The Radio Ministry

Although Helena and I had every intention of returning to Angola and viewed our time in Brazil as temporary, the civil war that broke out, which went on to last thirty years, prevented us from doing so. At the beginning of every year during my time at seminary, I would hope and pray that would be the year we would see an end to the civil war, so I could return to my beloved country. I could never have imagined the different plan that God had for me and my family. The Bible says in Proverbs 19:21, "Many are the plans in a person's heart, but it is the Lord's purpose that prevails." I was about to see this verse become a reality in our lives.

In 1976, during the second year of my theology degree, the director of a ministry called Trans World Radio came all the way from São Paulo to talk to me. I had never met this gentleman nor heard of his ministry so I wondered what would cause him to make such a trip. I soon found out that he was sent on assignment by a church in Angola called Igreja Evangelica Sudoeste de Angola (IESA) and a ministry called Swiss Alliance Mission. They wanted to know if I would be interested in preaching the gospel to Angola through the Trans World Radio ministry.

He explained that I would be trained on how to prepare and record the messages and on how to operate all the equipment in the recording studio. I told him that I liked his proposal but as far as training on how to prepare messages, there was no need because I was already studying hermeneutics and had preached at churches in Rio and São Paulo. The director was kind enough to look past my arrogance and say, "There is a big difference between preaching from a pulpit and preaching on the radio. When you preach from a pulpit, you are preaching to a visible audience in front of you, and you can see by their response if your message is having an impact. You don't so much preach on the radio, as talk to a person who is on the other side of the world, in adverse places and circumstances. It's more of a heart-to-heart conversation where you use your imagination. While directing your message to a single listener, you are actually speaking to millions of people at the same time." I liked his explanation and quickly realized that I knew nothing about the inner workings of speaking on the radio. The director handed me the official invitation, and I asked him to give me some time to talk to Helena and pray about it.

Helena encouraged me to accept the offer, but I still had some reservations because I didn't fully understand the ramifications of preaching the gospel on the radio. I kept thinking that if I dedicated my life to the radio ministry, then I would be isolated and no longer have fellowship with a congregation as their pastor or with my fellow pastor friends. I decided to talk to a friend of mine, the same one who had gone with me to pick up my suitcase when I first arrived from Angola.

He listened as I told him about the proposal and my reservations and then said, "This invitation is a great opportunity for you to reach your people from right here in Brazil. God is calling you to return to your people through your voice, because the possibility of you physically returning to Angola right now is basically nonexistent." He concluded by encouraging me to accept the proposal. It didn't take long for me to realize that God was using him to confirm something similar the Trans World Radio director had said to me. From then on I started to get excited, and every time I thought about the invitation, it was no longer with fear and uncertainty, but with peace and joy. I soon called the director to let him know that I would gladly accept his invitation and that my written acceptance letter would be in the mail in about a week.

I traveled to São Paulo for training and on October 10, 1976, I recorded my first ten-minute message in my native language, Umbundu. I was so nervous that I was shaking. The technician that recorded the message had to make me stop and repeat parts of it several times, and it took an hour and twenty minutes to record the fifteen-minute program. The program was entitled "Sanjuka," or "Be Happy" in English. Besides the message, the program had an introduction, announcements, a musical interlude, and closing remarks. In the end, the program turned out really good; so good that while listening back to it, I was able to imagine myself as a listener back in Angola who was dealing with the circumstances of the civil war. I became emotional and couldn't contain the tears of joy for what I had been able to accomplish. As far as I was concerned, there was no doubt that this was the ministry that God had for me and my family. When the technician saw the tears flowing down my face, he put his arm around my shoulders and said, "These tears are a sign that we've done a good job."

It wasn't until I started recording the programs that I began to understand what had initiated their ministry and the inner workings of getting them on the air. The Igreja Evangelica Sudoeste de Angola (IESA) church in Angola, in partnership with the Swiss Alliance Mission (SAM), invited a Swiss missionary couple to go to Angola, with the goal of starting a radio ministry. This ministry would produce fifteen-minute programs in the Angola native language of Umbundu.

The couple accepted the invitation and quickly got to work building a recording studio at a mission compound in the town of Cassua, training recording technicians, and teaching pastors how to prepare messages and preach them on the air. Groups of young people were also taught to play different musical instruments and sing worship songs that were, and are still, used for the programs. Once ready, the programs were sent to Luanda, and then to Swaziland, Africa, via regular mail. Over time the missionary developed a friendship with the gentleman at the post office that was responsible for processing all international mail. This man was an instrument from God during many years in ensuring that the programs arrived safely in Swaziland.

Several years later, the missionary couple and their children had to return to Switzerland because of the civil war that broke out. The studio was then moved from Cassua to the city of Kalukembe, which was also where the IESA church has its headquarters. From then on, it became extremely difficult to send the programs to Swaziland.

There was a period of time when the tapes with the programs were taken by missionaries who traveled from Kalukembe to Switzerland and then sent them to Swaziland from there. Once, a courier was carrying programs recorded on reels of tape from Angola to Switzerland to give them to the director of the Swiss Alliance Mission. The director was waiting to receive them at the airport in Zurich so they could later be sent to São Paulo. On the train from the airport, the director put the reels of tape in the luggage compartment above his seat. He got off the train and realized that he had left the reels behind, just as the train was taking off. Trying hard not to panic, he went to inquire about when that train would be passing through that station again on its return voyage. Since it wasn't any time soon, he had to sit at the station and wait for several hours. As soon as the train stopped at the platform, he hurried in and was relieved to find the reels exactly where he had left them. God had kept them safe and His protection and faithfulness were manifested in a visible way that day.

Later, the tapes started being taken to the Trans World Radio office in São Paulo by the director there, who would travel to Switzerland often. I would then take the tapes, copy them to a K7 tape format and would mail them to Swaziland to be aired via shortwave to Angola. It was a complicated and rather long process but we were all committed to delivering the gospel and did whatever was necessary.

The Trans World Radio director in São Paulo later invited another pastor from Angola, who also spoke Umbundu, to record programs as well. He had moved to Brazil with his wife and three sons to escape the war. Since he lived in São Paulo, it was easy for him to go to the studio and record his messages. He would record one program a week, and I would record two. These were then mailed to the Trans World Radio branch in Swaziland.

This setup was successful and continued for several years until we started to get resistance from the authorities in Angola. In seeing the positive effect that the program was having on the people, especially the soldiers, they decided to try to stop it by claiming that the messages were political. They of course were not, and the authorities had no way of proving their allegations. By this time, the program had a huge audience and in order to save it, we decided to change its name from "Sanjuka," "Be Happy," to "*Yeva Ondaka,*" "Listen to Word," and it continues to be aired under that name to this day.

Of the fifteen years that we lived in Brazil, ten were dedicated part-time to the radio ministry. I would travel once a month to São Paulo and stay at the Trans World Radio studios for a week where I would work day and night and sleep right there in the studio so I could record all the programs for the following month. When I couldn't travel because of classes or exams at the seminary, I would use the studios at a Baptist church in Niteroi, near Rio de Janeiro, to record on Saturdays. The programs were recorded on coil tapes and were then sent to São Paulo to be copied to cassette tapes before being mailed to Swaziland. The pastor had graciously told me that he wouldn't charge anything for the use of the studio or any technical assistance. He said that it would be the church's contribution to proclaiming the gospel to the people in Angola.

As I continued recording multiple programs, I eventually ran into a problem. Since I only had a couple of songs in Umbundu to use during our musical interlude, I had no choice but to keep repeating them. Needless to say, the listeners soon grew tired of hearing the same thing. That's when I had the idea of turning five Brazilians, who were members of our church in Rio, into a small choir, and train them to sing in Umbundu. We began practicing every Wednesday night after midweek service. When the time came to start recording the music, we would travel to São Paulo on a Friday night, record about eight songs in the morning, and make a U-turn right back to Rio de Janeiro that same night. Our time in São Paulo was intense and the traveling exhausting, but it all worked out surprisingly well.

When I launched the songs for the first time in one of the programs, I announced to the listeners that the music they had just heard was courtesy of their Brazilian brothers and sisters in Christ. Positive feedback soon began rolling in from listeners thanking us for the choir, and their efforts of singing in a foreign language with only the slightest hint of an accent. To my surprise, word of our "Umbundu" singing choir got out and began circulating among churches in the Brazilian Baptist Convention. An article was even published in the *Baptist Journal* with a picture of the choir, and a caption that took Acts 16:9—"Come over to Macedonia and help us"—and adapted it to "Come over to Angola and help us." I read the article and was humbled by the words describing what we had worked so hard on and were able to accomplish.

Listeners not only liked the new music but the messages as well, and soon the program's audience base began to grow. The signal that goes out from Trans World Radio in Swaziland is extremely powerful and covers the entire nation of Angola. The *Yeva Ondaka* program was heard by individuals from all different social levels, especially by the military who were fighting in the fields.

The impact of the program, and the way that it started transforming the lives and characters of its listeners, was astounding. Letters with powerful testimonies started pouring into the station in Swaziland. They came from all over Angola but especially from refugee camps in Zambia, Namibia, and South Africa. Since there wasn't anyone at the studio in Swaziland that spoke Umbundu or Portuguese, all this mail was sent to São Paulo for me process. It was a hard and time-consuming task because I could only do it once a month during my recording visits and the listeners had to wait a long time before they received a reply from us.

With the civil war and the oppressive political system that the people were facing, they were hungry to hear the word of God. We received many questions during that time, including a heart-breaking one that was all too common: "If God is love, then why is there war in a country where Angolan citizens are killing their own brothers? Why would God allow something like that?" Giving a biblical response to this and other questions like it was not easy.

> *"The Spirit of the LORD is upon Me, Because He has anointed Me To preach the gospel to the poor; He has sent Me to heal the brokenhearted, To proclaim liberty to the captives And recovery of sight to the blind, To set at liberty those who are oppressed; to proclaim the acceptable year of the LORD."*
>
> —Luke 4:18-19 (NKJV)

Ministry as a Pastor in Brazil

My introduction to the pastoral ministry came in 1979 in Mococa, a small country town a few hours' drive from São Paulo. Mococa is a town that is fiercely Catholic and therefore not easy to evangelize. To try to reach the citizens with the gospel, I passed out tracts on the street, and went door to door. I also set up a children's ministry, which included Vacation Bible School, that helped encourage parents to visit our congregation on Sundays.

While doing some door-to-door evangelism one day, I came across this huge house that had two ferocious dogs who took their guarding duties very seriously. I cautiously knocked on the door, intending to give the residents a flier with the message of the gospel. A gentleman who appeared to be around fifty years old opened the door. I introduced myself as new to the city and that I wanted to give him a flier with the Word of God. He quickly noticed my accent and asked where I was from. I told him about my origin and he became so interested in finding out more, that he tied up his dogs and invited me in. As we sat and chatted in the living room, I found out that he lived alone and that his grandparents had immigrated to Brazil from Italy.

We spent some time talking about Angola and the Portuguese colonization in Brazil and Africa. Eventually, I handed him one of my fliers and started to share the gospel with him. As soon as I mentioned the Bible, he asked that we change the subject because he hated the Bible and Christians as well. He went on to say, "I was offered a Bible by someone from a Christian church, and to be honest with you, I only accepted because I didn't want to be rude. I don't believe in it or in God. I was so angry that this Bible was now in my possession, that I put it in a pot with water and boiled it that same day. Then I took the liquid and drank it. I was so furious that I wanted to die. I honestly don't know how I'm still alive."

I told him that he was still alive because God loved him and had a purpose for his life. He said that the protestants and priests were all hypocrites because they talked about God but didn't practice what they preached. I quickly realized that it would be wiser not to continue the conversation. Something told me that this man knew some less than honorable things about the people in town, especially the ones who called themselves Christians. I asked instead, "Would it be all right if I prayed and left this flier with you?" To my surprise, he said yes. I bowed my head and began to pray, "Father, I ask that you bless this gentleman, and that you reveal Yourself to him in a very special way. Please show him Your purpose for his life and take away this anger that he has against Christians and your Word. In Jesus's name, amen."

When I finished, he told me that he liked the prayer and that I was welcome to come back whenever I wanted. Although I did return a few days later, I didn't find him and it was months before I eventually ran into him again in town. He recognized me instantly and walked over to greet me. Apparently, he had moved to a city nearby called São João da Boa Vista and was in town to sell his house. With the biggest smile on his face, he then shared the wonderful news that he accepted Christ after reading the flier that I left for him, and that he was now just waiting to be baptized. I was delighted. I gave him a big hug and prayed with him right there on the street.

God completely transformed this gentleman through His Word on that flier. I was reminded of a valuable lesson that day: that my responsibility as a pastor is simply to sow the seed of the Word of God. The growth of that seed and its spiritual fruit is the Holy's Spirit's responsibility. It wasn't easy winning souls in Mococa but this gentleman's conversion always served as a source of encouragement for me. By God's grace, we were able to take a small group of Christians that were meeting every week, and officially start a church with forty-three members.

A few weeks after the church was launched, Helena and I received an invitation from a church called Grace Baptist in Belo Horizonte, in the state of Minas Gerais. I had met the pastor of that church several years prior during a conference where he was the main speaker. I was still in seminary at that time and as I was introducing myself to him, I told him about my fiancée who was arriving from Angola in just a few months. I shared with him Helena's desire to get a music degree at the seminary where I was attending. To my surprise, he told me to make sure that Helena registered for classes when she arrived, because his church would be willing to pay for her studies. True to his word, the church faithfully covered the costs of Helena's education every year for four years. So, when we received the invitation to move from Mococa to Belo Horizonte, it didn't come as a surprise. Not only did we know the pastor and this church well but they were near and dear to our hearts. By this time, Helena and I had already started sensing that our time in Mococa was coming to an end so, we gladly accepted the invitation. Besides, as missionaries and church planters, we also wanted to experience new evangelism opportunities in other states.

The invitation from the church in Belo Horizonte was

for us to serve as their missionaries by planting a church in what was then an underdeveloped neighborhood called Ceu Azul. When we arrived in Belo Horizonte in December of 1980, the first challenge we faced was the size of the apartment that the church had rented for us. We were coming from a big house in Mococa, with the amount of furniture to match. So, when we walked into our new accommodations, we quickly realized that our possessions were about to undergo some serious cutbacks. The apartment was tiny and there was barely any room for our daughters to play. It was a major adjustment, especially for Helena who stayed home with the girls all day. Yet in spite of it all, we were very happy with our new assignment. The challenges simply helped us mature and further develop our attitude of gratitude for everything we had. Within a year, we were able to rent a bigger, three-bedroom, apartment in that same building. Needless to say, we were all delighted. We could finally have guests over and the girls could play freely to their hearts' content.

The congregation in Ceu Azul met in a large room that the church in Belo Horizonte rented and the members consisted of more children than adults. I used the same one-on-one and door-to-door evangelism method that I implemented in Mococa. One of the great things about the people in that neighborhood is that they welcomed visits from pastors. There was a general level of respect for pastors, as the people saw them as servants of God who came to bring blessings to their homes and families. We could go to someone's home without having gone through the formalities of setting a date and time and be instantly welcomed. The people were so hospitable that they wouldn't let us leave without making sure that we had eaten something first. After a couple of these visits, I learned to pace myself, since I was expected to eat something at every house where I stopped. Because I would usually make these pastoral visits in the afternoon, I also had to make sure to leave room for the delicious meals that Helena would prepare every night.

I enjoyed making these visits and with the passing of time, I began to see my efforts start to bear fruit. There were instances where couples were having marital problems and God used these visits to strengthen them, or other times where children did not have good relationships with their parents and God used me to help them talk and develop mutual respect. God also used these visits to help their unsaved family members to trust the church and pastors in general, as they saw for themselves the positive results of us being there. Some even went on to ask us to visit their own homes. This building of relationships and trust between us and the community made it easy for us to invite them to services and for them to accept. Ultimately, many lives were changed by the power of the gospel and the congregation grew spiritually and in numbers. We soon outgrew our location and the church in Belo Horizonte and, with the financial help of a Baptist church in the United States, bought some land and built us a new sanctuary.

Speaking at the National Directors and Chaplains Meeting of Baptist Schools in Brazil

While I was busy pastoring, our daughters were attending the state branch of a college that belonged to the National Baptist Association. I got to know the director at the college fairly well and one day he surprised me with something totally unexpected. He extended an invitation for me to serve as the school's chaplain. I must admit that the prospect did not thrill me as I had several reservations. First, I would be replacing a pastor friend of mine, who had years of experience as a chaplain. This was the same pastor whose church had helped pay for Helena's studies and who had invited us to move to Belo Horizonte. We were good friends, and he had confided in me the different challenges of being a chaplain at the school. Then, there was the fact that I had no training in being a chaplain. And finally, the school had a total of eight thousand students in their elementary and high school. I would have to preach to an audience of about a thousand every day and my messages had to be effective and concise as they couldn't exceed ten minutes. In addition, the preaching schedule included a message to the high schoolers four times a week, and another for the teachers twice a week.

Helena and several friends, including the director of the school, encouraged me to accept the invitation. It was, after all, a great opportunity to permeate the students' minds with the Word of God. So, after putting my reservations aside and genuinely seeking the will of God, I accepted. Time has helped me realize that even back then, God was preparing me to step out into territories that were outside my comfort zone. But more on that later.

In accepting this position, I added more responsibility to my plate and also some much needed income to our household. Due to the state of the economy at that time, it was a challenge for most families to live on just one salary. Helena and I were not exempt from this challenge and we both had to work. In my case, that meant multiple jobs. I was the chaplain at the school, taught theology at the seminary at nights, and I was pastoring the church. Helena started teaching music at the seminary. Even with both of us working, what we brought in at the end of the month wouldn't always cover all of our expenses comfortably. Thankfully, one of the advantages of working as a chaplain at the school was that our daughters were able to attend tuition-free. Even though we struggled with paying for school supplies and additional costs, which were not cheap, the fact that we didn't have to worry about tuition made a huge difference.

Balancing all three jobs was often a challenge, especially since my responsibilities as chaplain were complex. The chaplain ministry extended beyond the students to their families. Whenever there were problems of bad behavior with any of the students, the school would have me visit the parents and talk with them first before calling them in for a meeting. In many instances, the bad behavior was a result of relational problems between the student and their parents. The parents would often tell me that they both worked and the demands of their jobs would leave them little time to spend with their children. Since it was fairly inexpensive to hire help back then, many families had maids or nannies that would take care of the children. They were the ones we saw bringing the children to school and picking them up later.

When I would visit the students' parents, along with praying with them, I would also recommend that they visit the counseling department at the school. Our counseling department was very good and many students, as well as their parents, benefitted from it; some even came to the Lord through it. My duties as chaplain also had me visit students and parents in the hospital and even perform funeral services for a parent or a close family member.

I could share many stories about the different people I had to visit and their situations, but there is one that had a lasting effect on me and stands out most of all. There was a doctor who had two sons who were students at the school. He discovered that he had cancer and that it was already at an advanced stage and the medical report indicated nothing more could be done for him. Yet despite this hopeless prognosis, he was still seeing patients part time in his office. Medicine back then was not as advanced as it is today and there was no treatment or medication to help prolong his life and delay the inevitable. About that same time, I had written an article in the school's newspaper to honor doctors on National Doctor's Appreciation Day. In the article, I commended doctors on their incredible work and dedication and expressed our gratitude to them, stating that we owed them much. I also spoke about Jesus as the ultimate doctor, from whom we could receive strength, courage, and healing for our bodies and souls.

The article was given to all the students whose parents were doctors, and this doctor read one of the two copies that were brought home by his sons. The next day, I received a call from him, asking me to come to his office. I did so the following day, not knowing at the time that he was sick. When I arrived and we sat down to talk, he said how much he liked my article. He went on to tell me about the cancer and how he was blindsided by it because he felt no pain until it was too late. He then said, "I feel so alone. Few of my friends take the time to come and see me. I never really thought about God, never had the time really because I was always busy treating others. Now I've got this terminal illness and I can't treat myself. Your article has made me stop and seriously think about God." With a sadness in his eyes that I will never forget, he asked me what he needed to do to be saved. I told him about the love of Christ and the power of the gospel and then prayed with him. I followed up by sending him a Bible but just as I was thinking of going to visit him a couple of weeks later, I received the news that he had passed. It saddened me that he was no longer with us, but I was grateful that he had accepted the Lord's gift of eternal life.

When I went to the funeral, I was touched to see the Bible that I had given him laying on top of his coffin. I picked it up and noticed that several passages were highlighted, especially in the New Testament. His widow came over and told me how her husband would read that Bible nonstop and how he was able to peacefully face death. She said how grateful she was for all the spiritual help that our department provided and for my presence at the funeral. I left that day feeling grateful for the privilege of being God's servant in helping the students and their families during difficult times.

My time as a chaplain lasted seven years, and these weren't without their challenges. There were some who said that I wasn't the right person for the job because I was a foreigner. It wasn't easy knowing that people thought that, and there were times when I was tempted to resign. What helped me were testimonies like the one I just shared and the changes I personally witnessed in the lives of the students, their parents, and the teachers. These were a great encouragement for me not to give up but continue in my task with determination and faith. God also used this experience to help me grow professionally. My goal was always to be a counselor and a promoter of God's peace and love. I can humbly say that to the best of my ability I was able to do that, and when I left my position at the school, I did so with no complaints or grievances for the work that I had done.

> *"So shall my word be that goeth forth out of my mouth: it shall not return unto me void, but it shall accomplish that which I please, and it shall prosper in the thing whereto I sent it."*
> —Isaiah 55:11 (KJV)

Becoming Brazilian Citizens

While living in Belo Horizonte, a crisis arose for Helena and I that left us disoriented and uncertain of our own identity. When Helena and I left Angola for Brazil back in 1975, we did so with a Portuguese passport that was valid for four years. So, when Angola gained her independence, we were left with documents that were no longer valid and no Angolan embassy in Brazil to update them. Since we couldn't remain undocumented, I decided to go to Angola to get new documents and a passport.

Before leaving, I obtained a document from the Brazilian government that allowed me to leave and re-enter the country. With all my paperwork in hand, both Angolan and Portuguese, I traveled to Angola thinking that the immigration department would accept the original documents I had since that would have been the logical procedure in most countries. Imagine my surprise when after landing in Luanda and going through immigration, I was banned from entering the country because I had "left at the most critical time when your country needed you." Since they wouldn't recognize any of my documents, and without any valid documentation, they kept me locked up at the airport for two days without food. I was able to get word of my situation to Helena's family and they allowed my mother-in-law to bring me some food. Meanwhile, one of Helena's uncles was able to get me a temporary document that allowed me to enter the country and stay for fifteen days.

Knowing my delicate situation, I didn't waste any time and took the opportunity to visit my family and some Christian leaders, along with going to the respective governmental offices to try to get Angolan documents. My attempts to legalize my status were futile as I was repeatedly told that I may have been Angolan by birth but as far as being a citizen, I no longer had that right. The reality that my own country had disowned me simply because I had left at "the wrong time," finally sank in.

When I boarded my flight back to Brazil, I was depressed, despondent, and felt like an orphan. By the time I landed, I was so angry that I rushed home and told Helena that we should forget about Africa, especially that wicked country of Angola. Helena was surprised by the intensity of my anger but was equally frustrated with the new government that had left us with no country to call our own. Once the initial shock and anger wore off, we decided to petition the Portuguese government for a conversion of citizenship. Apparently, we were even less desirable to the Portuguese, and they responded by saying that our ancestors had nothing to do with their nation. Helena and I couldn't believe that after being colonized by these people for over four hundred years, they had the nerve to say we had nothing to do with them? Forget the fact that all our legal documents had their official seal on them. I look back now and realize that had we not received encouragement and reassurance from the Lord that He would take care of the situation, both Helena and I would have reached the depths of despair.

The only option left to us was to apply for citizenship to the nation that had embraced us. We sought a lawyer and began the process of petitioning for Brazilian citizenship. In less than six months, we went from being permanent residents to official citizens. The fact that we had two daughters who were born citizen accelerated the process tremendously. Helena and I were extremely relieved when this situation was finally settled and we didn't even know that God was going to use our new citizenship to help facilitate some things in the future.

> *"So then you are no longer strangers and aliens, but you are fellow citizens with the saints, and are of God's household . . . "*
> —Ephesians 2:19

Move from Belo Horizonte to São Paulo

The year was 1987, and after spending six full years as a chaplain at the school in Belo Horizonte, and pastoring two local churches, I started sensing that God was about to bring change our way once again. The Bible says in Ecclesiastes that there's a time for everything, and although my time at the school had been extremely fruitful, I knew that it was coming to an end. So, as I was praying and seeking the Lord about His next step for our lives, I received another life-altering invitation.

Throughout our time in Belo Horizonte, my trips to São Paulo to record my radio programs never ceased. The challenges of not having someone at the studio in Africa to help with the programs continued, and it was becoming increasingly difficult to produce all the *Yeva Ondaka* programs in Angola. The leadership was now looking for a permanent solution and it came in the form of an invitation for my family and I to move to Swaziland. There, I would serve full-time as producer and general overseer of programs to Angola in the Umbundu language. Our move to Swaziland appeared to be the only logical option to continue the programs that had become so well-known and beloved by the Angolan people and those who lived in neighboring countries.

We would need to move to São Paulo for two years first so I could be trained as a studio operator, thus enabling me to record my own programs. This move would mean an enormous change and adjustment for the whole family, especially for the girls. It would require us to leave our friends, our church family, the school, and everything we had grown to love and call home. We would be leaving our comfort zone for a missionary position in a country that most people had never even heard of.

Even though I had been sensing that change was coming, it was a serious struggle to come to terms with and accept this invitation. Truth be told, I was happy pastoring a church and thought I would continue to do so full time, if not there, then somewhere else. When Helena and I finally accepted that this was to be our new assignment, I announced it to the school and the church that I was pastoring. People were shocked. They thought we were crazy and that I was making a rash decision. I was told by many not to leave because going full-time into the radio ministry would isolate my family from contact and fellowship with a church body and would isolate me from fellowship with other pastors. Sound familiar? Others reminded me that I was over forty and this was not the time to be making drastic moves or venturing into new ministries. All thoughts that had passed through my mind at one time or another. Thankfully, there were also those who said that if God called me to preach the gospel in Africa, then I should step out and not look back because the same God that made the call would also take care of me and my family.

With all these different opinions and my own fears and uncertainties, it wasn't easy doing what I knew was right for me and my family. But with Helena's support, I officially accepted the invitation and in February of 1987, we moved to São Paulo. Unlike our initial move to Belo Horizonte, where we were greeted with tiny living arrangements, the ministry rented a big house for us that was close to the Trans World Radio studio. We enrolled our daughters in a school near the house but adjusting to this new school was not easy for them especially for our oldest. Helena did a wonderful job in encouraging them and doing whatever was necessary to help minimize the impact of all these changes.

I was at the studio from 8:00 to 5:00 p.m., where I would spend the mornings training and the afternoons recording new programs. My salary was not enough to cover the expenses of our household, so Helena took a teaching position at a private school. This school was mostly attended by students from affluent homes and some had serious discipline problems. It was difficult for Helena to find a balance between keeping order in the classroom and not crossing a disciplinary line that went beyond her function as a teacher. She would often come home exhausted and would sometimes cry out of frustration. By the grace of God, she pressed on and worked at that school for a year. She only resigned when it was time for us to make the move to Africa.

After we had been in São Paulo for about two months, I received an invitation to become the pastor of a small church where the previous pastor had some serious moral shortcomings, resulting in the departure of many members. Some moved to other churches while others decided to forgo church all together and stay home. The latter justified their decision by saying that there was too much hypocrisy in the church. I knew I would have my work cut out for me by taking this on, but I decided to accept the invitation. My main goal was to win the unsaved in the neighborhood and try to bring back those members that had left. I started visiting the old members right away and soon realized that very few would be returning. Most of them were reluctant to go back to a church where they had experienced offense and difference of opinion with the previous pastor. The bottom line was that the church had lost all credibility in the neighborhood and people didn't want anything to do with it.

Of the four churches that I pastored in Brazil, this one was the most difficult but also the most rewarding. God used Helena and I to help heal the wounds in the church and help the members become a unified body once again. The church came back to life, and we had youth and young adults that were dedicated and passionate for the things of God.

Eventually, we were able to invite people from the neighborhood to our services and they would accept without reservations because God helped us rebuild the integrity of the church. Helena was instrumental during this process, not only with her support as a pastor's wife but as the pianist and music director at the church. We were so beloved by the congregation that when we announced our move to Africa, the members were really upset, and some even tried to persuade us to stay. But we had a divine calling, and in February 1989, we left Brazil and, much to Helena's content, the red refrigerator and stove as well.

> *"Blessed are the peacemakers, for they shall be called sons of God."*
> —Matthew 5:9

Part 3
Launch and Development of the Ministry in Swaziland

The Move to Swaziland

Swaziland, which in 2018 changed its name to Eswatini, is a small country in the southern part of Africa. It is landlocked between South Africa and Mozambique and was once a British protectorate. There are still strong ties between the two nations and, like the United Kingdom, Eswatini also has a monarchy. The difference is that their prime minister is not elected by the people but nominated by the king. This results in the king having almost total power in the decision-making process and ruling of the country. The country is known for its game reserves and natural beauty. It's often referred to as the Switzerland of Africa, due to its mountains, valleys, and other geographic similarities. Along with the national dialect of Siswati, English is also spoken. The capital, called Mbabane, is one of the country's two major cities with Manzini, its commercial and industrial hub, being the second. It was in this small kingdom, in the city of Manzini, that Trans World Radio International built its recording studios from which the gospel is proclaimed to surrounding countries via short and medium wave antennas.

Before we traveled to Swaziland, we had to obtain a work permit in order to enter the country and live there. Funny enough, when it came time to send our documents for our upcoming move, we were told that our Brazilian passports were ideal for traveling throughout Africa because many countries were not accepting the Angolan passport due to the governmental system in place after independence. So, what had previously been a problem and an offense to our dignity, God later used and worked out for our good. With everything in order, we boarded our flight from São Paulo to Johannesburg and after an overnight layover, we boarded a forty-five-minute flight to Swaziland.

On the day we landed at the airport, which was just outside of Manzini, we were met by several missionaries who came to welcome us. It was a wonderful surprise, and we were very thankful because it gave us a sense of not being alone in a strange land. They drove us to an apartment where we would stay until our house became available as there was a missionary family in the process of vacating it to return to the United States. This apartment was next door to a missionary couple whose wife spoke Portuguese, and she became our lifeline to our new surroundings. The ministry also set up a system where fellow missionaries brought us dinner every night for our first week there. Everyone went above and beyond to ensure that we felt welcome and that our transition would be as smooth as possible.

Yet despite all this care and attention, we still had many challenges. For starters, our two daughters, Djamila and Priscila, who were twelve and nine respectively, did not speak a word of English. They had to learn it before we could enroll them in school; but thankfully, an American missionary who had been a teacher, taught them for three months. To help with the learning process, they also set up "playdates" with other missionary kids so they could interact with others and strengthen their conversational skills. Eventually, they were given the green light to be enrolled in school.

My and Helena's English was not much better. Although we had attended English classes during our two-year "layover" in São Paulo, what we learned left us with little more than the ability to order a glass of water. Over time, we became more fluent as we talked with our coworkers and fellow missionaries. Since everyone spoke English at the office, this helped us a great deal, but unfortunately, it also limited our exposure to the native language of Siswati, which we never learned.

Another challenge was the city of Manzini itself, which was small in size and population. We had come from a big metropolitan city and, at that time, São Paulo had a population of about ten million people. Manzini's was seventy thousand. Life there was slow and monotonous. The city would be deserted after 5:00 p.m. because people would leave work and return to their homes in the villages, which were usually far from the city. We often felt isolated, especially on weekends. What helped us during this time were the invitations for dinners at the other missionaries' homes. This was a common practice among the missionary community there, to facilitate communion among the families. With time, we developed an appreciation for the city and its people, so much so, that our initial four-year contract turned into a twenty-two-year stay. This again proved that the best place to live in the world is where God sends you, no matter the challenges.

Believe it not, getting certain items at the store was also an issue. When we arrived, the commercial embargo against South Africa was in full effect due to apartheid, and since products could not be officially imported from South Africa, they were simply not available. To add to the problem, we were landlocked and Mozambique, who was our other neighbor, was in the middle of a civil war. Not only was their help not an option but the limited items that they did have were worse than what was at our disposal.

The only solution was to personally go to South Africa and buy products, but even that had its challenges. There were serious restrictions because of their segregation system and we couldn't have a South African visa in our passport. If we did, then entering Angola, or some of the other African countries, became out of the question. We finally found a way around that by getting a multiple-entry visa that could be used as a document on its own. So, once a month, we could cross the border into South Africa and go shopping at one of the nearby towns. Although this was inconvenient and took time and gas money, we gladly did it and returned with a car full of provisions for the month.

Whenever you move to a new area, security is often a factor that you have to consider. This was the case for us when we moved to Manzini, but nothing could have prepared us for what we were about to face. A few months after we moved to our house in Manzini, it was broken into on a Sunday afternoon while we were visiting fellow missionary friends. The thieves took everything that they could carry. Although the mission made a point to install alarm systems in all their houses, ours never went off. It appeared that the job was done by individuals who were familiar with that system and were able to deactivate it soon after their entry.

I had a small wallet with 350 dollars that I kept in a drawer, hidden under some books and papers. As the thieves searched for valuables, the wallet fell and ended up under the bed. When we arrived back home and were doing an inventory of what had been taken, the wallet was the first thing I looked for. I couldn't believe that I found it and that all the money was still there. Once again, I realized that God had shown His protection and care toward us, even in circumstances that were hard for me to comprehend. He protected us by ensuring that we weren't home when the thieves broke in and that the things that were taken could all be replaced with the $350 dollars that He hid from their sight. It amazed me that in the fifteen years that we lived in Brazil, this never happened to us. Then we move to a sleepy town that would lose half its population on weekends and are robbed. When I wrote to an elderly friend in São Paulo who often prayed for us, her faith was shaken because she couldn't understand why God would let this happen to one of His servants. I told her that even as missionaries, we still lived in a world where the enemy reigns through violence and that we are all subject to the same trials as unbelievers. The difference is that we have the presence of God with us to protect, guide, and provide everything we need when faced with difficult circumstances. Needless to say, this was a traumatic ordeal for all of us, and I'm sure that Helena and the girls were wondering about my decision to bring them there. But the Lord brought us through it; and in time, fear stopped overwhelming us, and we were able to move forward.

Finding a church to attend in the mission field can be a challenge, but in our case, not in the way one might think. Upon our arrival, we quickly learned that the missionary community was attending one of two churches. Neither were Baptist. In fact, the only Baptist church in the country was in the capital city of Mbabane, which was forty-five minutes away. Since you could cross the city of Manzini in under five minutes, anywhere that took forty-five might as well have been another planet. The Baptist church was not an option. So we settled into one of the two local options and started attending faithfully every Sunday.

To look at us, you would have thought we were the picture of the command in the Bible for Christians to "not forsake the assembling of ourselves together," but the truth was, we were more like the popular saying of "Fake it 'til you make it." We attended, but we understood little of what was preached or said by the pastor or Sunday school teachers. The mental strength it took to understand what people were saying left us with a headache.

I remember one particular Sunday when the pastor told us to turn to the book of Micah, and Helena and I turned to each other with blank looks on our faces. We had our Portuguese Bibles with us and absolutely no clue of the corresponding book in our language. Eventually, Helena asked a lady sitting next to her for help, and by noticing the book of Jonah before it, we figured it out. Since our daughters learned English faster than we did, they eventually became our translators, and helped us until we could fully understand what was being taught. I believe that the Lord honored our efforts of sitting through those services during those early years, especially since it would have been easier, and less stressful, to just stay at home.

Another challenge arose when it came time for our daughters to graduate from elementary school. The only option for high school in Manzini was an all-girls school run by the Catholic church, so all the missionary children would attend a high school in the capital city. The mission had a house there and a missionary couple took care of the students and served as house "parents." The students would stay there all week and come home on weekends. This setup had been in place for some time and worked well until some of the missionary families started leaving the mission field and there were no longer enough students to justify keeping the house or the parents. By the time Djamila entered her final year of high school, she was the only one that remained and we were left with a crisis.

When we asked some of our friends in Brazil to join us

in prayer about the situation, some sympathized and stood with us while others told us that we were simply reaping what we had sowed by leaving Brazil and inflicting this disaster upon our girls. It was disappointing to receive such a negative response, but we continued to pray and seek the Lord. Ultimately, the only option we had was to join a carpool with a few non-missionary parents that made the forty-five-minute drive to the high school and back every day. Djamila's senior year was challenging for all of us. When it was time for Priscila to go to high school, the school in Mbabane was out of the question, so we enrolled her in a school about an hour away in a city called Big Bend. This was a boarding school where the students stayed in the residences during the week then returned home every weekend.

The education obstacles did not end at the high school level. When it was time for Djamila to go to university, we were once again faced with limited options. There was a possibility for her to study in South Africa, but with the end of apartheid and the government's decision to suspend the acceptance of foreign students to their universities, that door quickly closed. We considered leaving the mission field and returning to Brazil, simply to give our girls the best possible education scenario. While we prayed and waited for the Lord's leading, our daughter stayed busy helping in the correspondence department at Trans World Radio.

Eventually, God presented an opportunity in a most unusual way when we discovered, through one of the American administrators at TWR, a new work-study scholarship offered by Liberty University in the United States. The school would pay for tuition in exchange for 250 hours of work per semester, anywhere on campus. As we were encouraged to apply for the scholarship and fill out the paperwork, we were also warned that if she was accepted, we would still have to cover the cost of room and board, food, health insurance, and any travel expenses, which would amount to a lot of money. While pondering this option, we again asked our friends for prayers and received a similar response as before. Some showered us with emotional and spiritual support while others said we needed to come back down to reality because we were dreaming to even consider universities in the United States. Yet God answered our prayers by our daughter being accepted at Liberty and by us receiving support from a generous Swiss donor for all the other expenses. It wasn't easy for Djamila to move to another continent, or for us to be away from her, but we recognized the opportunity that God made available. When it came time for Priscila to go to university, she also became a benefactor of this scholarship and support. The interesting thing is that shortly after her studies were completed, the university stopped offering that scholarship.

In all of these and other challenges that we faced, we saw the hand of God guiding us. We learned the true meaning of living by faith and depending completely on Him. This continues to be true to this day.

> *"For we walk by faith, not by sight."*
> —2 Corinthians 5:7

Growth of the Ministry in Swaziland

Helena, working on follow-up correspondence from listeners and students of the Portuguese Bible Courses

The training I received in São Paulo turned out to be invaluable. There were four recording studios at the office in Manzini and few technicians to operate them. So those producers who knew how to operate the equipment and record their own programs could do so, since the studios were setup to enable that. I developed a routine of writing scripts for the programs in the mornings and recording them in the afternoons. There was a period of time when the church in Angola was unable to record new *Yeva Ondaka* programs and I had to fill in and produce more than my share. I became solely responsible for new programs for quite a while and was recording thirty of them a month. Eventually, the need to fulfill this quota came to an end, and I was relieved when the church was able to start recording once again.

We continued to receive many letters from soldiers and generals, high-ranking officials, and the average individual. They all shared how God was using the programs to transform their lives. Helena stepped in once again and helped me process all this mail. She would take care of the letters in Portuguese and the correspondence for the Bible courses that we offered, and I would take care of all the letters in Umbundu. One of the common responses that we received was from soldiers saying that the program brought them encouragement, comfort, and hope that the war would end soon.

I still remember a letter in Umbundu from a certain soldier saying, "The *Yeva Ondaka* program is teaching us about the love of God, acceptance, and forgiveness. I believe that the war will end and that we as a people will unite and forgive one another. We will also forgive our leader who instigated all this hate and the killing of thousands of soldiers and citizens. God is using the *Yeva Ondaka* program to prepare the Angolan people for this . . ." The letter was sent in 1993, and the war didn't end until 2002. Since then, there's been a great effort by the authorities and the people in general to overcome the ethical, cultural, and social differences and to become a loving and united nation. The negative consequences of the civil war were inevitable but were dealt with in a spirit of tolerance and forgiveness. I have no doubt that God used the *Yeva Ondaka* program as an instrument to sow this mindset in the hearts of the Angolan people.

"So, as those who have been chosen of God, holy and beloved, put on a heart of compassion, kindness, humility, gentleness and patience; bearing with one another, and forgiving each other, whoever has a complaint against anyone; just as the Lord forgave you, so also should you."

—Colossians 3:12-13

Clarity and the Four-Year Mark

Although we were missionaries in Swaziland at Trans World Radio, we were not the average missionary because we were working with, and under, Trans World Radio and the Swiss Alliance Mission. We would work in Swaziland under TWR and make programs that were supported by the Swiss Alliance Mission, which financed the *Yeva Ondaka* program. To add to this collage of organizations was the Igreja Evangelica Sudoeste de Angola (IESA) church who the Swiss Alliance Mission partnered with as well for these programs.

Even though this might seem like the ideal setup for confusion and misunderstandings, the system worked well for the most part with the exception of a few problems that arose and could have been avoided. One of the issues was that there wasn't a clear communications procedure set up between the three organizations, and this would often jeopardize their ability to flow in one accord. The main issue, however, was that we were never told who our official "employers" were once in the missionary field, so when it came time to address certain things pertaining to our future, this became a problem. But I'm getting ahead of myself so let me back up and explain.

When we arrived in Swaziland, it was under the understanding that our stay there would be temporary. In fact, we were told by the leadership at Trans World Radio in São Paulo that we would only stay for four years. This news filled our daughters with hope that they would soon return to all that was dear and familiar to them but it also led to our decision to leave some special items in storage at friends' houses. One such item was a beautiful custom-made oil painting of a shepherd with one of his sheep, which was given to us by the church we pastored in São Paulo.

As we drew close to our four year mark, I decided to speak to my leader at Trans World Radio about the necessary arrangements for our return to Brazil. With a look of surprise and confusion, he asked me who told me that we would only be staying for four years. He went on to say, "Truth be told, what you should be preparing for is 'furlough.'" I was shocked, but that quickly gave way to thoughts of what this news would do to Helena and our girls. How in the world was I going to break it to them that not only were we not returning to Brazil anytime soon, but we were now expected to take a lengthy trip, to parts yet unknown, in order to raise support for an extended stay in Africa?

Helena had a similar reaction to mine when I told her the news later that day. The truth was that we were both blindsided, and it took us a while to wrap our heads around the fact that instead of Swaziland being a temporary assignment, it was our home until the Lord told us otherwise. The girls cried when we told them and accused us of knowing all along and tricking them into moving there. Ours was not a happy home for some time. Funny enough, when we did go on that required furlough a few months later, it turned out to be a wonderful trip for us as a family and a great experience for the girls. We ended up traveling to Switzerland in December of 1992 and were there for two months. When we returned, Helena and the girls were at peace with our new reality, and I was invigorated and ready to move forward with the work of the ministry.

"The mind of man plans his way, But the LORD directs his steps."
—Proverbs 16:9

Ministry with Refugees from Mozambique

Mozambique was a Portuguese colony for many years. Like Angola, the people spent years fighting for their independence; but after obtaining it, the nation was thrown into a civil war against the socialist-communist government that rose to power. This led many of its citizens to seek refuge in neighboring countries, especially Swaziland, since the two nations shared a border. When we arrived in Swaziland, there were two refugee camps: one in Malindza with a population of about fifteen thousand, and the other in Big Bend with a population of about twenty-five thousand. These two camps were forty and seventy kilometers from the city of Manzini, respectively. The refugees included women, children, young adults, and men. There were instances where entire families had to walk away from everything, including their homes, lands, and animals and would cross the border with little more than the clothes on their backs.

When I went to the refugee camp for the first time, I was shocked and disturbed by the poverty and conditions that the people were living in. On my way back home, I kept thinking about what I could do to help these people who were enduring such suffering. As a preacher on the radio, I was busy in the studio during the week, declaring the gospel to my people in Angola. On Sundays, however, I was often frustrated that I couldn't do the same for the people in Swaziland because I didn't speak their language and barely spoke English.

One day, a South African couple came to our church on

a Sunday morning. After the service, they invited me to go with them to the camp in Malindza and help distribute clothes and fliers with Bible verses. It was during the distributions of the fliers that I sensed an inner voice say, "Isac, you are frustrated at not being able to preach the gospel on Sundays, and here are people suffering without salvation, that speak your language. Share the Word of God with them." As we made our way back to Manzini, I shared my experience with the couple and asked their opinion on the possibility of me starting Bible studies with the refugees. They were elated and encouraged me to start right away and said they would send more fliers for me to use. I told Helena as soon as I arrived back home and she also encouraged me to move forward. Unfortunately, Helena wouldn't be able to accompany me on Sundays since she was one of the organists at our church, and she also had to take care of the girls.

With a strong conviction that this was the will of God, I went to the authorities to learn what the legal procedures were on starting a church at the refugee camp. I was informed that I needed to get written permission from the king. With the help of a friend, I got all the documents that were needed, including all my personal documents and a solicitation letter. Once submitted, the process had to first go through the United Nations department of refugees before reaching the desk of the sole ruler of the country. Miraculously, I was granted permission to start the Bible studies in both refugee camps in just four weeks. I honestly believe that part of the reason my petition was approved so quickly is due to the convictions of the king and the citizens in Swaziland who consider their country to be a Christian nation, even though their strong traditions and customs sometimes override biblical principles. Since they house the short-wave antennas that proclaim the gospel to several countries in Africa, the Swazi people take pride in calling their country "Africa's pulpit." The other reason, I believe, has to do with the support that the king gives to the churches encouraging them to teach the Bible to his people.

With my acceptance letter in hand, I decided to focus on the camp in Malindza first, since it was closer to Manzini. I started out my first Sunday by sharing the gospel with the people one-on-one. By the time I reached my fifth person, I found a fellow believer who had distanced himself from God and the church because of the war. He was a young twenty-seven-year-old man, who had heard the gospel through a Brazilian missionary who lived in Mozambique for eleven years. He had accepted the Lord nine years before and was now living in the refugee camp to avoid being forced to join the army and fight in the civil war. He had already lost his older brother in the war and was totally against all the fighting among their fellow brothers and citizens.

Although this young man was disillusioned with the things of God, he didn't object when I suggested we start studying the Bible together in his tent on Sundays. Before we started, we would go throughout the camp and speak to the people about Christ and invite them to join us. There was a lot of need there, especially for food and clothing. The Swazi government provided these things, but it was never enough because every month brought new arrivals. All that need and suffering caused the refugees to seek God, and we saw several individuals give their lives to Christ every Sunday, including professing Muslims. Our Bible study group grew rapidly as the people were hungry to hear and study the Word of God.

There were many among the refugees who were extremely angry, and some would come to disturb our meetings by standing outside yelling that what they needed was food, clothes, and money, not the Bible, and that I should stop the services. I immediately sought the help of the authorities at the camp, and not only did they encourage me to continue but they did everything in their power to ensure these disturbances stopped. One of the authorities was especially supportive because he was a member of the Nazarene church and strongly believed that the Word of God would change the character and behavior of the people. Once the authorities got involved, we no longer had problems with disturbances, and the people continued to grow spiritually and in numbers.

Missionaries from various organizations praying for the refugees

In less than six months, we had fifty new converts at our meetings, which were held under a tree. I knew we needed a more appropriate meeting place, especially since we had to cancel service during the rainy season, so I asked the authorities to provide a large tent for us, but they quickly informed me that they didn't have one. Our group then suggested I ask for a plot of land instead so we could build a church out of sticks and straws. Although the authorities were able to provide the plot, they would not allow us to cut down any trees to build because they were few and far between. I spoke to the group and suggested that we pray and ask God to provide the finances for us to buy wood and sheets of metal to build.

About three months later, a Christian gentleman from Switzerland came to Swaziland to visit his daughter and son-in-law who were fellow Trans World Radio missionaries. They were friends of ours and they invited us to their house for lunch so we could meet the father. During the meal, I told him about the radio ministry to Angola and the work at the refugee camp. He was so intrigued that he asked to go with me to the refugee camp that following Sunday. We had a wonderful, anointed service under the tree that Sunday, and he was impressed by the work and growth of the church. On our way back to Manzini, I was surprised and overjoyed when he said that he would send me some money for materials to build the church as soon as he returned to Switzerland. The surprise continued when I received the funds and realized that he sent enough to build two churches, one in Malindza and another in Big Bend.

The amazing part of all this was that one of our new converts had worked in construction back in Mozambique, so he took on the responsibility of buying all the materials, preparing the land, and building the church. He also became the head of a construction committee that we set up. Under his hard work and leadership, we were able to build a two hundred-seat church in Malindza and Big Bend. The church was simple with seats made of planks of wood that were nailed to wooden stakes, but it was also the only solid structure in the camp so it drew a lot of attention. The people were fascinated by the novelty of it all, and the church grew even more. In less than a year, we no longer had any space to accommodate all the people that would come to hear the Word the God. Our Sunday schedule would begin with Sunday school at 9:00 a.m. and a service at 10:30 a.m. Baptisms would take place every fourth Sunday in a plastic swimming pool that an American missionary loaned to us.

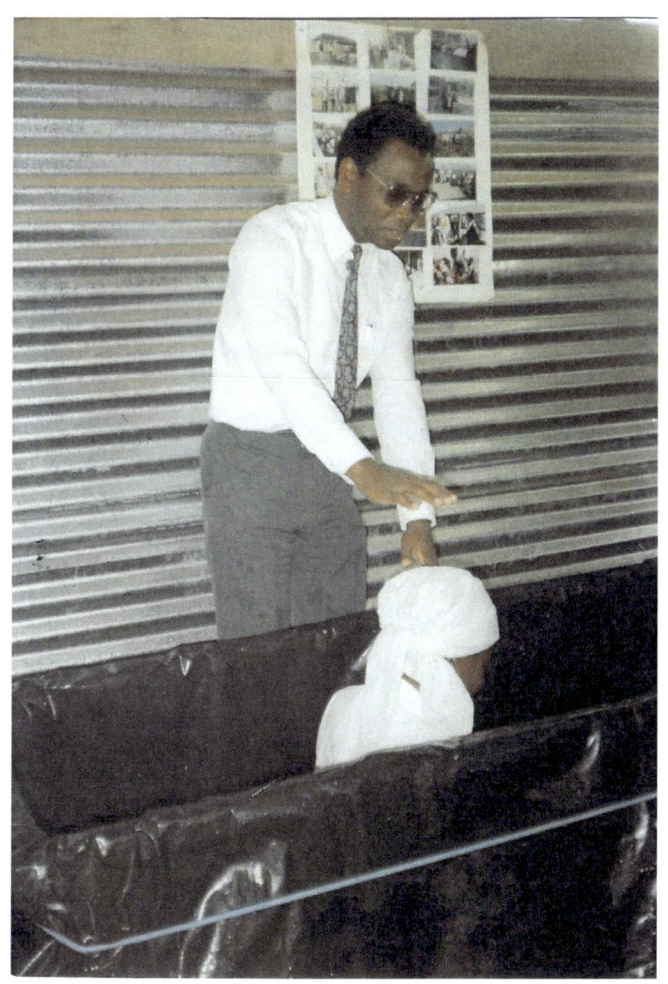

Baptizing believers in the portable swimming pool

It's not unusual for people that are suffering and have great material needs to accept anything that might help them without considering the consequences. We witnessed such cases with several refugees who turned to the occult, thinking that it would help alleviate their suffering and protect them. Thankfully, some of these individuals were also drawn to the church, heard the gospel, and gave their lives to Christ. They were freed from the enslaving power of the devil and willingly surrendered everything they had previously used to defend themselves against demonic attacks and curses or get "favor" to obtain material things. Others also surrendered occult items that they used to attack and kill their enemies. On several occasions, we had to burn these items after the service.

Burning witchcraft paraphernalia

At the end of my third year of working in Malindza, I chose ten men who showed leadership skills and trained them to take over in the event that I was unable to go on Sundays. I also instilled in them the vision to plant new churches when they returned to Mozambique, as they would have the one in Malindza as an example. The men excelled in their training and this gave me the liberty to start working at the other refugee camp in Big Bend.

Church and ten trained leaders at the Malindza refugee camp

After almost four years of ministry at the two refugee camps, the civil war in Mozambique finally ended in October of 1992, and the refugees were able to return to whatever was left of their previous lives. Although many left, others preferred to stay in Swaziland, where they had learned to start over and build new lives. By then, our church had grown to a congregation of four hundred members and ten leaders who were trained and ready to start churches of their own. We wrote letters to the authorities asking them for permission to take down the two churches and for transportation for the leaders to take the building materials back to Mozambique with them. The authorities granted our petition and also wrote letters to the officials at the border to ensure that the materials crossed over with no problems and without taxes having to be paid. As a result, ten churches were started in seven different provinces, under the covering of the First Baptist Church of Maputo and the Baptist convention in Mozambique.

Although my work at the refugee camps was challenging and entirely voluntary, it was also filled with many spiritual rewards. The feeling that I got of having accomplished a mission for God brought me a lot of peace and joy. When I later visited one of the leaders that had planted a church not too far from the border, he thanked me for allowing God to use me to bring him to salvation in Swaziland. He went on to say that he felt like the Psalmist when he said, "It was good for me to be afflicted so that I might learn your decrees" in Psalms 119:71. It was worth it for him to have suffered for four years as a refugee in Swaziland so he could find Christ and be used to proclaim the gospel to his people. God went on to use him to start seven churches in three hard to reach provinces. To this day, we still stay in touch and talk on occasion.

When the Swiss gentleman returned for a second visit, he formed a nonprofit organization, recognized by the Swazi government, to help fund evangelism and the distribution of Bibles. As its founder and president, he named it the Bible Evangelism Fund (BEF). His son-in-law and I were part of a nine-member council, and I was nominated and given the role of vice president. Since the president was unable to oversee daily activities and manage the organization from Switzerland, a majority of that responsibility fell on my shoulders as second in command.

The ten leaders from the refugee camps that started churches in Mozambique were "adopted" as missionaries by the BEF organization. They each received a token of gratitude every month for their work, as well as Bibles and fliers to help in their evangelism efforts. In the event that they needed to travel throughout the country on mission trips, the organization covered all their expenses. The financial help that BEF offered was not limited to just these leaders.

We also helped churches in South Africa, Swaziland, Namibia, and Mozambique to train new leaders by financing both bachelor and master's degrees in theology. Those that received these scholarships were first approved by their churches and then were evaluated by the BEF council through a series of forms that they and their church leaders had to fill out, along with an interview process.

By the time I left my post as vice president in May 2010, we had helped sponsor the training of 250 future pastors. Many of them are still pastoring today while some with master's degrees are teaching at Bible schools and others are serving as missionaries in various parts of Africa. The organization is still helping churches train leaders to this day, albeit in a lesser capacity.

Another area where BEF offered support was by helping the Swazi Trans World Radio employees buy their own land and build houses. At that time, Swaziland had a predominantly low-income population and the average salary was very low. BEF would function as a financial institution by providing low-interest loans, considerably lower than the average banks, which could be repaid in monthly installments. We would also offer these loans to churches who needed to remodel their sanctuaries or build new ones. It was always a pleasure for us to later visit these churches, that had previously held services in tiny buildings built with sticks and straw but now met in brick structures with roofs and cement floors. A pastor once told me that his greatest joy was to no longer have to worry about his church catching on fire and burning down.

It gave me so much satisfaction to be able to help the African people through our work at BEF, because we not only gave them material things but the gospel that has the power to change lives. When we moved to Swaziland, I understood that my family and I would not be there forever, so I needed to take advantage of any opportunity to serve the people while there was time. God gave me time, strength, and grace and enabled me to do just that.

> *"Then the righteous will answer Him, 'Lord, when did we see You hungry, and feed You, or thirsty, and give You something to drink? And when did we see You a stranger, and invite You in, or naked, and clothe You? When did we see You sick, or in prison, and come to You?' The King will answer and say to them, 'Truly I say to you, to the extent that you did it to one of these brothers of Mine, even the least of them, you did it to Me.'"*
>
> —Matthew 25:37-40

Founding of Trans World Radio in Africa Mozambique

Trans World Radio International had a strategic plan to establish the radio ministry in several countries in Africa, with Swaziland as its African base. Of the Portuguese-speaking countries in Africa, Mozambique was the first to benefit from the building of a recording studio and the training of producers and announcers for the programs. After their successful setup, Angola, Cape Verde, and Guinea Bissau followed. Establishing the radio ministry in Mozambique was easy and difficult at the same time. Building the studio itself was easy but establishing relationships with the churches once the studio was built proved to be a challenge. At the time, the country was in the middle of a civil war, and it was impossible to buy land for the studio since the political system dictated that all the land belonged to the government. So, Trans World Radio Africa found itself in a situation where they had money to build a studio but no land to build it on.

We got in touch with the leadership at the Theological Seminary of the United Methodist Church in the town of Laulane, and they graciously gave us a plot of land in their compound. The studio was then built under the supervision of an American missionary. Once completed, we invited leaders from all the denominational churches, along with the president of the country, to the inauguration. It wasn't until after the inauguration that we realized the serious error we had committed that needed to be fixed.

When we told all the pastors that the studio belonged

to the churches, and that they should send gifted individuals to come and be trained in production and presentation of radio programs, some refused to send representatives. They told us that they were not confident in doing so because the churches were not involved in building the studio and some were unsure and leery of the source of the funds for its construction. One leader spoke to me privately and said, "I'm afraid of getting involved because maybe this was financed by a foreign government agency, with the hopes of influencing and disrupting the political system in our country."

When we heard and understood that this was the sentiment of many of the leaders, we realized our error in not involving them in the building process. Needless to say, establishing relationships with the pastors became very difficult after that, and I was tasked with uniting them around the idea of the radio ministry in Mozambique. Thankfully, God changed their hearts, and we were able to produce and air several programs in different dialects. Today, Trans World Radio Mozambique has its own building in the city center of Maputo and an FM station called Capital Radio. The lesson we learned from this experience helped us a great deal in establishing the ministry in Angola and other countries.

> *"Behold, I send you out as sheep in the midst of wolves; so be shrewd as serpents and innocent as doves."*
>
> —Matthew 10:16

Angola

After twenty years of having Swaziland as the launching pad to produce and air the *Yeva Ondaka* program to Angola, the church leaders in Angola felt that it was time to start a Trans World Radio ministry there. This way more programs in other dialects of the country could also be produced and aired through the short-wave antennas in Swaziland. So, the executives at the Evangelical Alliance of Angola (AEA) and the Council of Christian Churches (CICA), petitioned the leadership of Trans World Radio International to set up a ministry in Angola. The proposal was approved, and I was nominated by the Trans World Radio leadership as one of two individuals to oversee this new project.

I began my task with a trip to Angola to see firsthand the political, social, and religious condition of the country. Getting a visa to enter the country turned out to be challenging since I was no longer an Angolan citizen and was traveling with a Brazilian passport. I had to go to the nearest Angola embassy, which happened to be in South Africa, and wait a week in Johannesburg for it to be approved. I couldn't simply apply for the visa and return home because the embassy would keep my passport while they waited to hear back from the higher-ups in Angola if they would grant me entry. Thankfully, they gave me a thirty-day single-entry visa and I was able to travel with my colleague to Luanda.

Church leaders from various denominations at the meeting to discuss the launch of the radio ministry in Angola.

During our first meeting with the leaders of AEA and CICA, we all agreed that this new branch of the radio ministry should include all the churches. This required us to have a meeting with every denominational church to get their opinions on this new endeavor. It was no easy task getting everyone together for a meeting in Luanda but seventy representatives from every province and denomination eagerly gathered to debate and discuss proposals. In the end, we presented a document to the Trans World Radio leadership that started out by stating the importance of radio as a communications tool to preach the gospel and that the *Yeva Ondaka* program should continue because along with proclaiming the gospel, it promoted peace and reconciliation among the citizens. The document went on to ask Trans World Radio International to help build two recording studios to facilitate production of new programs in other commonly spoken dialects and to help train new technicians, producers, and presenters to proclaim the gospel on the radio. Once the document was submitted and everyone agreed on the terms, a committee was formed consisting of members of the three parties: Trans World Radio International, AEA, and CICA.

It was difficult to acquire land to build a studio back then, so a decision was made by the committee that the studio in Luanda would be built at the AEA compound. Funds were raised, and we inaugurated the studio in 1996, a year after our initial meeting. The other studio was built in Lubango on the grounds of the Theological Institute there and its inauguration was in 2000.

The building process for both studios was very complex because some of the building materials were not available in Angola and had to be imported from South Africa. There was also the challenge of buying all the studio equipment abroad, having it shipped, and getting it through customs. We faced so much bureaucracy that on top of paying the custom fees, there were one or two "officials" that wanted "a little something" to help expedite the clearance of the equipment. They figured that Trans World Radio must have money since the equipment was being imported and that this was an opportunity to take advantage of that. Since we were not interested in giving them "something," little or otherwise, it would take days for the equipment to clear customs, requiring us to have a great deal of patience and determination. Eventually, all the equipment was cleared and the engineers from the studios in Swaziland were able to install them.

Training radio program monitors how to operate windup radios that would be used in the villages.

When it came time to start training new producers, we selected twenty-four men and women who were pastors and laymen to learn the art of producing programs, writing scripts, and speaking on the microphone. Much like my own initial training, they also had to learn not to preach at the listener but deliver the message as if it were a conversation. Of the initial twenty-four, sixteen completed the training successfully. The new producers enabled us to add programs in the language of Kikongo, Kimbundu, and Chokwe. These were all recorded and then sent to be aired from the antennas in Swaziland.

These programs had a huge impact on the people, especially those who were isolated in the forests because of the war. Later, other churches who ministered to the population that spoke other dialects such as Lunyaneka, Fiote, and Luchazi also asked to produce and air programs in these languages. Eventually, a system was put in place where the studio in Luanda produced programs for languages spoken in the northern part of the country and the one in Lubango produced programs for those spoken in the southern part. We had a total of seven programs in different national dialects and various others in Portuguese geared towards children, the youth, those in the military, women, and those with illnesses such as leprosy and HIV.

When the director at the national radio station in Luanda, where we aired four of our programs, saw the success of our lineup, he gave one hour of free airtime to the churches. This allowed the whole country to be covered with the airwaves of the gospel from Swaziland Monday through Saturday, as well as programs in four national dialects on Sunday nights, on the national radio station.

Many individuals who listened to the programs, both in the cities and in the rural areas, would testify of the radical transformation in their lives and the impact of the Word of God. Those who were already saved were encouraged to remain firm and steadfast in their faith and in God's work. Numerous soldiers and military officials, who were on the frontlines, were reached with the biblical message of faith, hope, and salvation. We would receive many letters from Zambia, and the Igreja Evangelica Sudoeste de Angola (IESA) church went on to plant several churches there. I believe that these programs and the radio ministry is what helped to establish these churches because the IESA church became known through the *Yeva Ondaka* program. The leaders who went to Zambia found the people ready to receive the gospel without any hesitation because the radio programs had gone before them to prepare their hearts.

Every time I would travel to Angola, I made a point to visit the churches, and it was amazing to see the people's reaction when they realized that I had come from

Swaziland and was the one who oversaw the programs in the different languages.

I remember a particular trip to Luanda where I went to visit an old friend of mine who had become a general in the armed forces. During our conversation, he thanked Trans World Radio for airing the programs in Umbundu. He said that the program helped the soldiers to have hope that the war would end soon and that the people would reunite to create a better nation. He then asked me to follow him to a big room, and when he opened the door and turned on the light, I was surprised to see that it was full of Bibles.

"The radio ministry has given us faith and hope," he said. "We hand these out not only to our military but to everyone who comes to visit. Anyone who doesn't have a Bible has the opportunity to take the Word of God home with them." Words failed me, and all I could do was stare at the mountain of Bibles and the changed lives that they would represent.

After the general and I said our goodbyes, and as I was exiting the elevator, a sergeant walked up to me with a huge envelope in his hand and said, "This envelope contains letters from many soldiers who are in the woods and are listeners of Trans World Radio. We've been wanting to send them to Swaziland for some time now but didn't know how." I must confess that I was suspicious and hesitated in taking the envelope since the use of timed bombs in unassuming packages was common back then. The security guard that was accompanying me must have sensed my hesitation because he took the envelope and carried it to my car. When I arrived back in the room where I was staying, I opened the envelope and found over fifty letters inside. All were testimonies of how the messages in the programs had impacted the listeners' hearts and minds. Since the letters had no return addresses, and the subject matters were all so different, we had to reply to each one individually. Once the replies were written, they were all placed in a big envelope and hand-delivered to my friend, the general, so he could ensure that they were given to the right soldier.

Although it's been forty years since this branch of the radio ministry was started in Angola, it's important to point out that all of this was birthed as a result of the *Yevu Ondaka* program, which was founded by the couple who were missionaries of the Swiss Alliance Mission and the Igreja Evangelica Sudoeste de Angola (IESA) church. The ministry grew through partnerships between various Christian organizations and people who would manifest the spirit of cooperation and unity to further the common goal of declaring the gospel. This ministry helped unite the churches in Angola during a time when the country was going through the unprecedented struggles of civil war. Along with the churches in Angola, organizations such as the Swiss Alliance Mission, the IESA church, Trans World Radio International, Trans World Radio Brazil, Trans World Radio Africa, ERF, AEA-Angola, CICA-Angola, and SOLE-Angola were all key players that contributed to forming the ministry.

With so many different organizations, it wasn't always easy for me to navigate the partnership waters. It required a certain level of sacrifice, patience, love, and wisdom from my part. I can honestly say that I was able to do this not by any great skill or efforts of my own but because I was simply a willing vessel and the Lord used me to accomplish His purposes. By God's grace and the unfailing support of some leaders who I now also call friends, this ministry continues to declare the Good News of Jesus Christ.

> "He presented another parable to them, saying, 'The kingdom of heaven is like a mustard seed, which a man took and sowed in his field; and this is smaller than all other seeds, but when it is full grown, it is larger than the garden plants and becomes a tree, so that the birds of the air come and nest in its branches.'"
>
> —Matthew 13:31-32

Cape Verde

When it was time to launch the radio ministry in Cape Verde, I traveled several times to the capital city, Praia, to meet with different church leaders. Setting up a studio there was considerably easier because we didn't need to build one. The churches provided a space in a building belonging to the Nazarene church that we were able to transform into a studio. Programs in the languages of Creole and Portuguese were produced in the studio and aired by the local radio stations. Soon, the *Thru the Bible* program in Portuguese, recorded in Angola, also began airing on a station in the city of Praia.

The impact of these programs has been amazing. Even now, as I write this chapter, the producer of the *Thru the Bible* program in Angola continues to receive phone calls, SMS, and e-mails from listeners in Cape Verde, sharing how much they have come to know the Bible, Christianity, and the love of God.

Since Cape Verde is a desert and there is little rainfall, agriculture is limited. Many people are unemployed and live in extreme poverty, resulting in the youth getting involved with drugs, both for personal use and sale. Yet despite all the poverty, many would testify of having been set free from the tyranny and slavery that the devil had them in. Listeners would write in saying that Christ transformed their lives and, therefore, they had the greatest wealth in the world. Others would write and say that they didn't understand the true significance of faith in God until they heard the gospel, and it helped open their hearts to the God who created and sustains the whole world.

The churches in Cape Verde are doing an amazing job

of proclaiming the gospel and the Trans World Radio studio has helped them produce programs that reach the population in hard-to-reach areas in the mountains and valleys.

> *"The thief comes only to steal and kill and destroy; I came that they may have life, and have it abundantly."*
> —John 10:10

Guinea Bissau

Much like Cape Verde, setting up studios in Guinea Bissau was also fairly easy. I traveled to Guinea and contacted missionaries from the Baptist Convention in Brazil, who had a local radio station in the city of Bafata. Instead of building a studio, our plan was to partner with ministries that were already in place and join forces in the work of radio evangelism. We had the programs ready, and all we needed was airtime at local radio stations. There were a couple of Christian programs on the air back then but nothing like the verse-by-verse Bible study style of the *Thru the Bible* program.

Unfortunately, the partnership with the station in Bafata didn't work out because its airwaves didn't reach the capital city of Bissau, where most of the population lived. We ended up partnering with a church in the capital city and through them we acquired airtime at the local radio stations. To this day, the partnership still stands and the programs continue to be aired. We also got involved in helping an American missionary who was building a training and discipleship center in the rural area of the country. He reserved two rooms in the building which he turned into recording studios where radio programs in the creole language were produced.

After I finished helping establish the radio ministry in Guinea Bissau, I flew back to Johannesburg and was blindsided by news of the sudden death of my boss, the international director of Trans World Radio-Africa. He died of a heart attack at a time when all the national directors for TWR-Africa were in Johannesburg for an annual conference. I arrived from Guinea Bissau and that night, he and some of the directors were meeting in one of the rooms at the house where I was staying. When the meeting ended, I came out of my room to greet them. The other directors came over to speak to me but my boss remained standing under a tree by himself. I walked over to speak to him and quickly noticed a look of sadness in his eyes. I had no idea what was causing it, and he never mentioned it. We spoke for only a few minutes and then he said his goodbyes and went home.

The next day, we received the news that he was gone. It was a shock and severe blow for me because along with being my boss, he was also my friend. He was a dynamic leader who was a visionary and a man of God. He led his subordinates with love and would bring correction without offending, give direction without humiliating, and valued integrity of character. I can honestly say that the man had no enemies. He founded Trans World Radio in Africa from Nairobi, Kenya, helped it grow, and expanded it to other countries in Africa.

With the loss of my boss, my work as director of programs for the African southern region became very difficult because I felt like an orphan who had lost his father. During this difficult time, I worked hard at trying to encourage the national directors, who were extremely discouraged by the loss of our leader. Eventually, with the support of new leadership at Trans World Radio, I was able to continue to advance and grow the ministry in each country, encouraging local churches to embrace the radio ministry as their own and contribute to it financially. It was a challenging time for all of us, one that demanded a lot from me personally.

"And I heard a voice from heaven saying unto me, 'Write, Blessed are the dead which die in the Lord from henceforth': 'Yea,' saith the Spirit, 'that they may rest from their labours; and their works do follow them.'"

—Revelation 14:13 (KJV)

Helena's Help and Ministry

Helena is a great woman of faith who commits and dedicates herself wholeheartedly to whatever she does. To see her flow in this capacity as she took care of our family and served in various ministry roles was not surprising to me because I noticed these special qualities in her when we first started dating. That's why I told her from the very beginning that I was going to be a missionary pastor. What I didn't realize then was that she also had a strong desire to serve the Lord and would often pray that God would use her in the music ministry at her church.

After we got married and I started pastoring in Brazil, Helena was always by my side, serving as minister of music at each church. When we moved to Swaziland, along with taking care of the family, she would work at the office in the mornings, overseeing the correspondence Bible courses that we offered to our listeners in Angola, Mozambique, Zambia, and South Africa. She also found time to be the organist at our church on Sundays and would often be asked to play at weddings and funerals. She did all of this without expecting anything in return because she saw it as a ministry.

After our daughters left home to study abroad, the leadership at Trans World Radio-Africa invited her to help launch a women's ministry called "Project Hannah" in Africa. Even though she had no formal training for the role, she immersed herself in the task of organizing prayer groups in the churches. With the support of their pastors, Helena encouraged the women to pray for themselves, their families, their churches and leaders, their government officials, and for the people in general. It wasn't easy for her to launch this ministry, especially since many of the churches already had their own prayer ministries in place. She had to first meet with the pastors of each church and then their female congregates and try to show them the benefits of going beyond their existing prayer ministry to join others from different denominations to form a prayer movement.

Her new role had a significant impact on me. When she first accepted this responsibility in 2001, I was the director of programs to the southern region at Trans World Radio. I received a great deal of support from her, not only as a wife but as a leader of a powerful prayer ministry. Her position granted us both the honor of having continuous prayer and intercession by the women for our responsibilities of traveling and meeting with various leaders and governmental authorities in the region. Whenever I would travel, I always had the privilege of preaching at local churches and on many occasions, several women would come up to me after my message, excited to let me know that they were members of the Project Hannah ministry and that they would often pray for Helena and I. Their joy at having the opportunity to do so touched me deeply.

Here is a brief account of Helena's experience in her own words:

>To write about how I got involved in the Project Hannah (PH) ministry, now called TWR Women of Hope, is to speak about my journey as a Christian and a missionary.
>
>I was still a teenager when I felt drawn to join the music ministry at my church. Years later, I obtained a formal education in music and became a music director. While in Swaziland as a missionary, and

leading the choir at my church, I felt the Lord leading me to something more but wasn't sure what that was. Months later, I was presented with an invitation to start a branch for the PH ministry in Angola. My immediate response was to decline because I didn't know where to start nor how to do the job. The other hindrance for me was the fact that I would have to travel frequently and flying has never been something I enjoy.

As I remained firm in my decision, Isac suggested I take some time to pray about it and then give my final response. A month after I started praying, I began to get excited about the idea of working with the women in Angola. I was also getting ideas on how to bring these women together and start a prayer ministry for them, their spouses and families, and for the country that was going through a civil war. This would be in addition to using the PH monthly prayer calendar, which included prayer requests from women around the world.

Before I accepted the invitation, I prayed and asked God to do the job through me and to allow me to simply be an instrument in His hands to do whatever He pleased. Just to give an idea on how He answered my prayer, my first meeting was with one of the pastors on a flight from Johannesburg to Luanda. The pastor was so excited about the ministry that he promised to speak to the director of the ladies' ministry at his church and organize some meetings for me. From there, the news spread rapidly, and I had more invitations to present the ministry to church leaders than I could attend. A year later, we started airing the Woman of Hope program, and that too was well received by listeners: Christians and non-Christians from all walks of life.

God did wonders through the ministry by bringing people closer to Him, setting them free from the snares of the devil, reuniting families, and strengthening churches. Personally, I also learned a lot and got to know God more intimately at a level I never imagined. God also used the ministry to prepare me for the next step of my journey with Him.

Like in every journey, the path is not always straight and smooth, nor is everything always rosy. Shortly after accepting the position, I learned that while I was the person chosen by the TWR South Africa leaders, the PH international leaders also had their own candidate and it wasn't me. Nevertheless, I labored passionately and tirelessly as a volunteer, expanding the ministry from Angola into Mozambique and Ivory Coast. The fact that the ministry was doing very well in those three countries slightly mollified the ill feelings of the party that didn't get their candidate accepted by the leaders in Africa. However, problems and tension began to manifest among the leaders, and ultimately started affecting me as well. Finally, after six years and seven months of ministry, I presented my letter of resignation. On December 31, 2007, I officially left the PH ministry.

Although Helena's journey with the Project Hannah ministry ended, God still had other plans for her to minister in an unexpected capacity in the future. But more on that later.

I am so grateful to God for the wife that He has given me, a faithful co-laborer of many years. God has given us the grace to overcome many of the challenges that go along with missionary life, and we have also experienced a great deal of joy and contentment over these years. Those who have been in the mission field know and understand this type of joy because regardless of the challenge, it pays to serve the Lord.

> *"And she never left the temple, serving night and day with fastings and prayers."*
> —Luke 2:37

Part 4
New Era of the Ministry in the United States

My Reinvention-Retirement

Shortly after my sixty-second birthday, Helena and I started thinking about the possibility of returning to Brazil to continue working until it was time for me to officially retire, which in Brazil is at sixty-five. With the end of the civil war in Angola, we started considering the possibility of moving there as well.

During our years of missionary work in Swaziland and in Brazil, we made payments towards the Brazilian retirement pension system, with the help of the Swiss Alliance Mission. So it made sense, and would certainly be easier, to move back to Brazil and retire there. We also figured that by moving back three years before my retirement age, I could still work a couple of years and we could reestablish old friendships as well as make new ones. We had developed many great friendships while in Brazil, but after living in Swaziland for so many years, some of those friendships fizzled or ceased to exist. We tried to stay in touch and even visit during our trips to Brazil every four years, but in some cases it simply wasn't enough.

Another aspect that made retirement in Brazil so favorable was the house we had there. A beloved friend and brother in Christ, who is in glory now, helped us build the house on a lot that we purchased before moving to Swaziland. As a builder and contractor, he graciously waved all his fees, and all we had to pay for was the building materials. He said that this would be his contribution for the missionary work we were doing in Africa.

The last and extremely attractive advantage of living in Brazil was that we would only be an eight-hour flight away from our daughters, son-in-law, and granddaughter, who were in the United States.

On the other hand, moving to Angola also had its advantages. We would be close to our extended family, we would be able to help the local churches and their leaders, and the radio ministry would benefit greatly by us living there as we could offer direction and stability for the future. Without a doubt this would be a great way for us to continue with the work that God was doing there and be an encouragement to some of our family members who had started drifting from the ways of the Lord.

Yet moving to Angola would also have its challenges. Angola was still struggling from the aftermath of the civil war, and we would have to adjust to living in a war-torn country, where getting everything from basic necessities to housing would be a challenge. Since we would be moving there as retired missionaries, finding a place to live would now be our responsibility, and buying even the simplest house or apartment would financially be out of the question. Back then, Luanda was considered one of the most expensive cities in the world to live in and to lease a basic two-bedroom apartment was $4–5,000 a month. This was way over the $2,000 we were expecting to receive from our pension and that was before all the transfer fees that the bank would impose. Being in Angola would also make it harder for us to see our daughters since there were no direct flights to the United States and any route we took would include a nineteen-hour flight, without counting all the layovers.

This was a difficult time for us as we tried to navigate the different options and seek the will of God. To add to our dilemma, the leaders at the Swiss Alliance Mission and a representative from my work in Angola went to talk to the leadership at Trans World Radio-Africa about the logistics for my retirement. To our surprise, the TWR director said that we had never been their missionaries and therefore they were not responsible for us in any way. Upon hearing these words, we were extremely offended and overwhelmed by the feeling of having been abandoned by the very ones who had benefitted the most from our years of committed work. With no clear path forward or reassurance of support from our current "employers," we began to worry. At times, we would become filled with anxiety and the only thing that got us through was the Word of God comforting and giving us hope that He was still in control of our lives and our futures. "Do not be anxious about anything, but in every situation, by prayer and petition, with thanksgiving, present your requests to God. And the peace of God, which transcends all understanding, will guard your hearts and your minds in Christ Jesus" Philippians 4:6-7. Time has allowed us to look back and see how much we learned during this season of uncertainty, and in the end, it strengthened our faith in the infallible Word of God.

While we prayed and waited on the Lord to give us guidance on our future, our daughters suggested that we include the United States as one of our options. They expressed their desire for us to be closer to them after being apart for so many years and mentioned that this would be the opportune time for us to be together again as a family. They went on to say that both our son-in-law and our granddaughter agreed with that sentiment.

We were excited and a little scared at this new possibility because although it would be wonderful for us to live near them, we were not sure that the money from our pension would enable us to do so. We also knew that finding work would be tricky because of our age. Our professional qualifications would probably have to be reevaluated and updated through some type of continuing education, and that would be challenging for us. The main obstacle though would be to obtain a permanent residence card from the US government, which we knew was no easy feat. We shared our concerns with our daughters but they insisted we apply for the card and wait to see what the Lord would do. They said we needed to really think about this as a serious option because there was going to come a time when we would need someone to take care of us, and who better to do that than them. We couldn't deny the logic in what they were saying, so when they sent us a list of the required documents, we started putting everything together.

Getting some of the documents turned out to be complicated, especially the criminal background checks for the three countries where we had lived. We had to travel to get the ones for Angola and Brazil because they required us to do that in person. We did all of this, all the while praying and waiting to see if this move truly was the will of God. Once we got all the documents together and our daughters filed the petition, it was amazing how quickly everything progressed. Within eight months, we received a notice requiring us to go for an interview at the US embassy in Johannesburg. There, they later finalized the process and stamped our passport to receive permanent residency status upon our arrival in the United States.

Since they told us we had to move within six months, we quickly got to work on selling our belongings and doing what was needed to close that chapter in our lives. Thankfully, most of our things sold quickly with big items like our car and furniture being bought by a work colleague and Trans World Radio respectively. The sale of the furniture turned out to be a blessing for us and Trans World Radio because we lived in the apartments above the office, which they planned on turning into a guest house. All we had to do was leave everything as it was.

Selling things was easy but as anyone who's had to move knows, packing can be a nightmare. Yet even in this, God helped and provided for us in amazing ways. A fellow missionary friend from Germany graciously gave us a large wooden crate that we used to pack pictures and other items that we were taking with us. We also received a referral for a reputable company that took care of transporting all our things to the United States. They did an amazing job of ensuring that everything was packed properly and it all arrived intact and without any problems.

It wasn't easy leaving our friends, church family, and the mission field after twenty-two years. It also wasn't easy to say goodbye to all those who worked with us in the various countries in the southern African region. Yet we had no doubt that our time there had come to an end and that God was calling us to serve from a different platform, one that also included reuniting with, and being closer, to our family.

We left Swaziland on April 20, 2010. The American embassy had given us all the documents for our immigration process, which had to be handed to an official at the airport when we landed. There was also an additional interview that we had to go through at the airport to get a temporary document to use until they mailed us the permanent residence card. I still remember how emotional and excited Helena and I were when we finished our interview and signed some final papers. My hands shook as I signed, not because I was nervous but amazed at how God had orchestrated everything for our move. The official noticed my shaking hands, smiled at me, and said, "Mr. Silvano, there's no need to be nervous. Welcome to the United States. This is now your new home."

When we finally left the immigration room and took the escalator up to the arrivals area, our family was there to welcome us with open arms. Our son-in-law drove us to their house and there was a big celebration that night. After years of living oceans apart, our family was finally reunited.

For a while, we experienced a practice that is natural in the Indian culture, where families with adult married children all live under one roof. Usually it's the married children that live with the parents though, but in our case, we were the ones living with our children. A month later, our permanent residence card arrived, granting us the liberty to live and work freely in the country.

> *"To every thing there is a season, and a time to every purpose under the heaven."*
> —Ecclesiastes 3:1 (KJV)

Culture Shock

One of the first things we had to adjust to was the dynamics of living with our children. No matter how welcoming and accommodating they were, at the end of the day we were still guests in their home. We had to be sensitive to their way of doing things, allow them to live their lives, and keep from interfering in family issues or imposing parental authority over them. After all, they were adults now and we were in their territory. It wasn't always easy for us to remember that and control ourselves in certain situations, especially when it came to their style of parenting our granddaughter. Yet we persevered and over time learned to navigate this new and often tricky territory.

Our son-in-law was wonderful throughout all this. He knew how to handle situations where our culture dominated and our language, Portuguese, could be heard the loudest. We never heard a single complaint from him nor did he ever make us feel like he was tired of having us there. One of the benefits that came from our time together was that we got to know each other as adults really well. When it finally came time for us to leave, and we apologized to them for our faults and mistakes, our oldest daughter said, "You don't need to apologize. You are both easy to live with." The fact that she could say that was a gift from God.

The twelve months that we stayed with our children helped us as parents because we were able to put into action the love that God intended to be shared among families. We also practiced self-control and respect by submitting to the leadership of our son-in-law as head of the house. It was by the grace of God that we were able to pass this test, and thankfully our family is still united and close to this day.

A challenge that surprised us was the need to adjust our mindset of community, which is prevalent in Brazil and Africa, to the American culture, which tends to be more individualistic and isolating. Making friends was not easy because we were accustomed to building close relationships, where you visit one another and get together often like family. Our efforts at trying to start friendships were often met by individuals who were looking to go no further than the acquaintance level. We have found that it is hard to establish true friendships in this society, even among brothers and sisters in the church. On Sundays, people greet and hug each other, sing and pray together, but after the benediction, it's every man for himself. True fellowship and communion are very limited outside of church. We tried to invite people to our house so we could sit and get to know each other over a meal, but very few accepted. There were even a few who asked us the reason behind the invitation making us feel like we had ulterior motives. We did, however, have a wonderful time with the few that did accept, and they let us know how much they too enjoyed the opportunity to get together, but we received no reciprocal invitation. Helena and I have come to understand and accept that as part of the culture, although this doesn't make it any less challenging for us to deal with it.

The home buying process was another learning experience for us. Considering how much easier it is to buy a house in the United States compared to other countries, Helena and I thought that getting a loan and buying our own home would be a piece of cake. We had no idea that we couldn't apply for a loan as new residents with no financial name or credibility in the country. On top of that, we arrived during the financial crisis that caused havoc on the real estate market, making the banks apprehensive of giving out home loans. The only way we were going to buy a house was by paying for it in full.

Since we didn't have that kind of money, our only option was to sell the house we still had in Brazil. While the United States was experiencing one of their worst real estate markets, the one in Brazil was thriving making it an excellent time to sell. The only problem was that the lady who was renting our house had just renewed her lease with no intention of leaving anytime soon. I had to travel to Brazil three times to negotiate with her and it took us a year to finally reach an agreement and sell the house. The silver lining in all of this was that while we were waiting, real estate prices kept dropping in the United States, and we were able to buy a very nice apartment with the money from the sale. The apartment is a gift from God because it's in a great neighborhood, is close to our church, and has all kinds of stores and restaurants within walking distance.

> *"I have become all things to all men, that I might by all means save some."*
> —1 Corinthians 9:22 (NKJV)

A New Era of Ministry in the United States

When we arrived in the United States, we started attending First Baptist Church of Atlanta. The church is known worldwide for its radio and television program, *In Touch*. Many people who visit or move to Atlanta go to the church to see for themselves what they have heard on the radio or seen on TV. Although we were familiar with the In Touch Ministries since Trans World Radio had aired the program for many years, we initially started attending First Baptist because that was where our daughters worshiped.

The church has thousands of members from various walks of life and origins. According to a church survey done back in 2016, there are over forty nationalities represented in the congregation. It's easy to see all this diversity too; one just has to look at the three hundred-member choir to notice the different races and facial features that help identify the national origin of individuals. With a church this large and diverse, it's easy to get lost in the crowd and become just a number. First Baptist is proactive though and does a great job of encouraging people to get involved and offers many different opportunities for everyone to serve.

When Helena and I decided to make the transition from attendees to official church members, we pondered which ministry to join in order to get plugged in and start assimilating ourselves to our new community. We ultimately chose the music ministry by joining the church choir.

It all started with us going to an "Open House" event

that the choir had. Although it was advertised as a "get to know" the members and observe a rehearsal, we quickly realized that the leader had every intention of turning every visitor into a choir member. After attending the rehearsals for four weeks, we took a test so they could determine our vocal range and assign us to a group. I was assigned to the second tenors and Helena to first altos. We were both a little nervous the first Sunday we had to sing but soon became comfortable and are now considered old pros.

Joining the choir has been a gratifying and eye-opening experience for me. I always thought that people in my age group shouldn't be singing in the choir because this was something best left to the younger generation. This experience has helped me realize just how wrong I was. I found myself surrounded by choir members who were not only seniors like me, but some were over ninety years old.

Our two-hour rehearsals on Wednesday nights are truly worship services. We don't just sing but pray for one another and try to meet any spiritual or material needs that may exist. On Sundays, we practice for twenty minutes and pray before singing in the two morning services. All singing is done from memory as we cannot have lyrics or sheet music in front of us.

Memorizing all this music can be challenging. As I write this, even though it's September, we have already started memorizing songs for the Christmas production, and some of them are nineteen pages long. Over time, I have developed a system that has helped me commit all these songs to memory, which in turn helps keep my mind sharp. Although demanding, all this time and effort is worth it, as we get to serve as messengers of God through music.

Along with becoming choir members, Helena and I later went on to join Sunday school classes and a prayer ministry that meets every week either in person or over the phone.

> *"For a wide door for effective service has opened to me . . ."*
>
> —1 Corinthians 16:9

Radio Ministry from the United States

Before leaving Swaziland, I made a point of traveling to Angola to say my goodbyes to family members, the churches I had worked with, and the leadership at the Trans World Radio branch. The leaders of the Igreja Evangelica Sudoeste de Angola (IESA) church in the city of Lubango arranged a special farewell service and invited the churches under the Evangelical Alliance of Angola and the Council of Christian Churches of Angola. There were over five hundred people in attendance. The service was very emotional for me because church leaders and the general public had the opportunity to testify how Trans World Radio was an instrument from God to support the churches and to take hope and salvation to places that could not be reached because of the civil war. Among the many programs aired from Swaziland, the one mentioned the most was *Yeva Ondaka*. The pastors said that there wasn't a single church in Angola who hadn't benefited from this ministry because those who accept Christ through it would ultimately come to the churches for baptism and membership. They also talked about the churches that were launched as a result of the program, many in areas with no congregations at all.

At the end of the service, the pastors asked me to think about the possibility of continuing to record programs from the United States. They wanted my voice to continue to be heard over the airwaves regardless of where it came from. I agreed to their suggestion even though I had no idea how I was going to make it happen.

Recording Studio in Atlanta, Georgia

A few months after arriving in Atlanta, I started looking for a studio where I could record the programs and send them to the station in Swaziland. With a spirit of service and the mindset of doing God's work without thinking about compensation or profit, I thought it would be easy to find a Christian radio station or studio that would donate an hour of free studio time to record my fifteen-minute program. All I needed was the studio, no technicians or operators since I was accustomed to doing it all myself. I was ignorant of the way things worked in the United States and soon realized that my hopes and expectations didn't align with reality. Nothing was free, especially when it came to radio and television. Maintenance costs for a studio were very high, and the cheapest offer I received for using one was $200 an hour. As a recent retiree, I had no way of paying that. I was naïve in thinking that they would give me the studio time for free because they were a Christian organization.

I got discouraged and had no idea what to do but the desire and enthusiasm to produce and record the programs persisted. In June of that same year, I went to a Trans World Radio conference with attendees from different parts of the world. Among them was a friend of mine from Australia who I met during our time as missionaries in Africa. We were delighted to see each other and used the intermission times to talk and catch up. During one of our conversations, I shared with him my desire to record and send programs to Swaziland and how paying for studio time had become a roadblock. He surprised me by suggesting that I set up a recording studio of my own at home.

"This would make your job a whole lot easier and wouldn't cost as much because all you would need is money for the equipment and installation," he said. "You would also be saving a lot of time and gas money by not having to go back and forth to the radio station." He went on to show me pictures of a studio that he had set up at his house and then helped me figure out what I would need to set up my own, which turned out to be around $2,600. I thanked him for the suggestion and told him that although I didn't have the money, I would work at trying to raise it.

Along with my Australian friend, I had an American friend at the conference that had also been a Trans World Radio missionary in Africa. We had worked together even though we lived in Swaziland and he in South Africa. We stayed at the same guest house during the conference and would wake up early every morning to pray and read that day's devotional from Our Daily Bread. When I told him about my conversation with my Australian friend, he encouraged me to move forward with the studio project. He said, "From what I know about the needs of the African people, your programs would really help the churches in the Portuguese speaking nations there." He went on to say that the lengthy civil war had divided the people, planted seeds of hatred among families, and destroyed the self-esteem of many. He also said the best way I could contribute to the restoration of human dignity, and bring hope for a better future, would be by continuing to proclaim the only thing that had the power to transform the peoples' lives. My friend's words not only touched me but encouraged me to have faith and pursue this idea of the studio.

A month after the conference, my Australian friend called me and told me that he had wonderful news. He had a check in his hands for the exact amount that I needed to set up the studio and would be mailing it that week. I was overjoyed and extremely grateful to God, and my friend, for the provision and had no doubt that I was on the right track. Everything was falling into place for me to continue to proclaim the gospel on the radio.

I was confident in the transforming power of the messages that were aired and what they did to change hearts and mold characters. I also knew the power that radio waves had in areas that were unreachable by pastors and other bearers of the Good News. Finally, I had no doubt that my messages of peace, reconciliation, hope, and salvation could still be used by God in a special way. So nothing could quench my enthusiasm and vision to move forward with the studio.

While Helena and I continued our search for our own home, I started producing messages from our daughter's house. The first one was entitled "Jesus is the peace for the World." To record it, I used a small portable recorder that I brought with me from Africa. I would take advantage of the quiet hours of the early morning and wake up at 4:00 a.m. to record. Initially, I tried doing it in the laundry room, but with the bad acoustics, I quickly gave up on that idea. Besides, the laundry room was directly beneath the room where we were staying, and my voice would carry and wake up Helena and the rest of the family. Eventually, I found a good place to record and got into a routine of recording a few messages a week.

> *"And every day, in the temple and from house to house, they kept right on teaching and preaching Jesus as the Christ."*
>
> —Acts 5:42

Purchase and Setup of the Studio

After we purchased our apartment in 2011, we decided to install the studio in one of the walk-in closets. It seemed like the best place for it since the closets here in the United States can reach the size of a small room. Before installing the equipment, I bought all the material needed to soundproof the closet and make it suitable for recording.

I was able to soundproof the future studio without any professional assistance because I had witnessed several missionaries set up studios in rural parts of Africa and paid close attention to their method. This enabled me to buy the material at a local retail store and do the work myself. I then bought an L-shaped desk with a glass top where all the equipment would go. When the room was ready, I started looking for a technician that could help me buy the right equipment and do the installation.

It wasn't easy finding the right person since we were new to the area and didn't know too many people. I started praying. Then one Sunday, I felt led to share with my Sunday school class my need for a technician that specialized in audio and recording equipment. I told everyone about the studio project and what I had done already to set it up. Some of my fellow classmates were amazed and promised to pray and help me find someone.

Two weeks later, a member who was absent on the day I mentioned the studio came to me after class and asked me if I had found someone. I told him that I hadn't, and he said that he was a technician and would be willing to volunteer his services. I couldn't believe what I was hearing.

God not only provided the right person but also someone who was willing to donate his time and expertise.

We scheduled a time for him to come to our house and see the space and he was amazed at how everything was set up when he saw it. The following week, we purchased the equipment, then he returned a few days later to install it. When everything was completed, he mentioned how happy he was to be able to give his work as a contribution to the radio ministry. He promised to take care of the upkeep and maintenance of the equipment for as long as the ministry continued and he remained in Atlanta. He did just that for five years and wouldn't allow us to pay him a single cent. In 2017, his company transferred him to England, and he offered to continue to do it long distance. Thankfully, the equipment has never given us any problems.

> *"But my God shall supply all your need according to his riches in glory by Christ Jesus."*
> —Philippians 4:19 (KJV)

Production and Recording of Programs

With the setup of the studio complete, I continued to produce and record the *Yeva Ondaka* program, as well as a new program in Portuguese.

Since the *Yeva Ondaka* program was aired daily, it was decided that I would record two programs a week from my new studio and the team at Trans World Radio in Lubango would record the additional five. All seven programs are then sent to Swaziland via Internet to be aired. *Yeva Ondaka* is also aired by the national radio station in Angola on Sunday nights. In addition, they also air four fifteen-minute programs during this time, that we provided, in four national dialects.

The director at the national radio station has mentioned that these programs helped the station broadcast the Angolan culture and motivated the people to master their national dialects. The Swiss Alliance Mission that birthed the *Yeva Ondaka* program continues to support its production and pay for the airtime.

Although production continues faithfully, there's a need to restructure the process and to train new producers and announcers. Some consideration also needs to be given to using other mass communication methods, such as the all-powerful Internet. Since the program is in Umbundu, the dialect spoken by the majority of the population, this restructure was necessary in order to reach the greatest number of people.

The new Portuguese program I started producing is called *Character First*. This program was birthed as a result of research I did when I traveled to a couple of cities in Angola and talked with several listeners. What I discovered was enlightening and motivated me to start recording.

The first thing I discovered was that although the short-wave signal from Trans World Radio in Swaziland was strong, it wasn't very clear due to various factors that interfered with the signal, especially in the capital city of Luanda. With the introduction and mass use of the cell phone, the new generation had little interest in tuning to a short-wave signal on a radio. They preferred FM stations and using their cell phones to access them. During a visit to Angola in November of 2017, I saw young people, on two separate occasions, listening to the local radio station on their cell phones. I asked one of them if he had a short- or medium-wave radio at home and he said only in his car. He went on to say that he rarely listened to those types of stations and preferred the FM station because it was easier to access and had a clearer signal.

The second, and very sad, thing that I discovered had to do with the different national dialects. The people I interviewed, men and women around forty years old, didn't speak the national dialect of their respective regions. The numbers only increased among the middle class and the affluent, especially in the city of Luanda. So, the programs in the national dialects were predominantly reaching the population that lived in remote parts of the country where the radio signal was strong and the dialects spoken daily. Realizing this deficiency, I decided it was necessary to have a program in Portuguese, targeting these individuals that were not being reached. So, *Character First* came into existence. The messages cover various topics that usually contain a brief scientific analysis, supported by the Word of God. The goal is to help the listeners trust God with their lives, families, and businesses and have perfect communion with Jesus Christ. Ultimately, create in them a hope for a future that will never die.

These messages started airing through local radio stations in Angola. Soon, a few church leaders from other Portuguese speaking nations started asking for the messages to be aired in their countries as well. Along with Angola, the messages are now also aired in Portugal, Brazil, and Mozambique. The program is not limited to radio only but is also available on the internet, and transcripts from the messages have been published in Christian magazines. With the goal of proclaiming the Good News of the gospel to as many as possible, my prayer is to reach all the Portuguese speaking nations.

There is an old saying that states that every generation ends up evangelizing itself. Looking from this angle, this places a great responsibility on my shoulders to ensure that those who speak my language have the opportunity to hear about the love of God and the saving grace of Jesus Christ. Without a doubt, God entrusted me with a great privilege when He called me to minister on the radio. I resisted at first, but the Holy Spirit convinced me to accept the challenge of sowing the good seed of the Word of God through the airwaves. I've enjoyed this wonderful experience of speaking to listeners in other parts of the world, even if I could only see them in my imagination. To be able to offer peace and words of hope to a person that might be lost and in despair is something indescribable.

> *"The things which you have heard from me in the presence of many witnesses, entrust these to faithful men who will be able to teach others also."*
> —2 Timothy 2:2

The *Virtuous Woman* Program

During one of our annual visits to Angola, some church leaders approached Helena about producing a radio program with short devotionals geared towards women. These devotionals would cover various topics that women deal with, especially issues within the family. Much like my own initial response to the radio ministry, Helena wasn't sure that this was a path for her. Although she had helped train producers and presenters during her work with Project Hannah, she had never been on the radio herself. So, she told the leaders that she would need some time to pray about it. Eventually, she accepted the offer and got to work. I tried to support her the best way I could and helped her put into practice the technical knowledge she already had.

Training Helena on radio production and recording

Here again is Helena with a brief account of her experience:

The next chapter of my life began in the USA. A year after we arrived in Atlanta, the Lord started to once again prepare me for a new step in my journey. At the beginning, I didn't understand why during my devotionals God would give me a complete message out of a Bible verse or a portion of scripture. Puzzled, I shared the experience with my daughter and asked what she thought. To my surprise she replied, "If God is giving it to you, then that means you will need it," and as it turned out, she was right. In early 2014, I received an invitation to start a radio segment for women, and in October of that same year, I started writing and recording the devotionals. These messages began airing in Angola and are now also aired in Mozambique and Brazil.

I feel honored and blessed by this opportunity to reach out to women from different backgrounds and cultures through radio. It was very hard for me at the beginning and I felt so inadequate that I thought of giving up. My first ten-minute devotional took almost three hours to record, as I had to redo it several times. By the end, my muscles were stiff and my whole body was in pain. Since then, I have improved a lot and am enjoying what I do. Frequent readings of the Bible, commentaries, and books on subjects I write about have enriched my own personal life.

There is a geographical aspect of this ministry

that can be challenging though. Because we live so far away from our listeners, I sometimes wonder if the messages are having a meaningful impact on the people, and then discouragement starts to set in. That doesn't last long though, and I am grateful for the feedback I receive from listeners and the occasional meetings I have with some of them.

We have seen the Lord use these devotionals, which Helena later named *Virtuous Woman*, to touch the lives of many. With their foundation of biblical scriptures and examples, the messages awaken and encourage the women to deal with their situations from a positive angle, one they might not have considered before. Others are drawn to such a personal relationship with Christ that it influences their spouses to consider Him as well.

There are few programs on the radio in Angola and Mozambique that deal specifically on issues that women face. So we feel that this program arrived at the right time to help them. In preparing these devotionals, Helena is aware of the differences in culture and traditions in every country. She also knows that the problems women face in these countries are more similar than they are different. The difference is in how they deal with them within the structure of their culture and traditions. That's where wisdom in leading the listener to look to God and His Word comes in, as He is the only lasting solution to their challenges regardless of their nationality, race, or social status.

I have the honor of also being involved in this process. When Helena records, she doesn't have to worry about the technical aspects because I take care of it as her studio operator. She simply comes into the studio, we pray together, and she starts recording. I later edit the messages and send them to the different stations via Internet.

It has been a gratifying experience for me to work alongside her in the radio ministry. We feel united, not just as husband and wife but also in our common goals and personal convictions. With the help of the Holy Spirit, we can see the paths that we need to take together in order to serve our Lord and Savior.

> "Older women likewise are to be reverent in their behavior . . . teaching what is good, so that they may encourage the young women . . . ."
> —Titus 2:3-4

Working from Home

One of the advantages of retirement is the ability to work from home when I want and at the pace that my body allows. I quickly realized, however, that if I didn't set a flexible schedule each morning, I would end up producing very little since there's always something to distract me around the house.

There's a destructive mindset that often plagues retirees, where they believe they now have unlimited time at their disposal. This is true for those who don't want to do anything else with their lives, who spend their time lying around on recliner, watching television or doing nothing at all. In some countries, like Brazil, some retirees spend their days walking around, drinking, smoking, and playing card games at the local parks.

As a Christian, I recognized that with my God-given gifts and strength, I could still contribute to society by helping people live in harmony and peace with one another through a personal knowledge of the Prince of Peace. So it was obvious to me that I couldn't squander the time and studio that the Lord had given me. At the beginning, there were days that I would work in my pajamas. I would waste time on things that weren't a priority for my life, my family, and certainly not for God. I didn't know how to manage well the twenty-four hours that were at my disposal. I would wake up and start doing one thing, then something else would come up and I would abandon my original task. The day would end with me not having completed anything. I had to correct my ways, and I decided to reorganize my day. As a habitual early riser, I continued to wake up around four in the morning, but the first thing I did when I entered the studio was make myself a schedule with items listed in order of priority. Naturally, the first item on my list was always spending quality time in God's presence. This system worked wonders and I still make these schedules daily.

After spending time with the Lord, I work for a couple of hours and stop for breakfast at some point during the morning. When I do stop, I normally take Helena a cup of tea in our room, where she's usually reading her Bible or other devotionals. I respect her space because that's her time to meet with God. She's always been a woman of prayer, and I know that she uses this time to pray for our family, the ministry, and for the needs of others. It's also during this time that she gets revelation, inspiration, and wisdom to write messages for the *Virtuous Woman* program. What better way to support and serve her than with a cup of her favorite tea? I then go back and work until noon, when I'm called to partake of the meal that Helena has lovingly prepared for us.

My afternoons are usually set aside to help with whatever is needed around the house or for personal errands such as shopping, paying bills, exercising, or swimming at the gym. I also take a nap to rest my mind and renew my strength. I do all these things within my physical capacities at my age. To sit around and do nothing is not an option because it wouldn't be good for me physically or mentally. As the old saying goes, "An idle mind is the devil's playground."

Working from home can be gratifying if the retiree knows how to maximize their time and abilities to benefit God's purposes, their society, and family. This is what I try to do every day, preparing for the day when my journey here comes to an end. My goal is to try to fortify the spiritual, moral, and material legacy that I wish to leave for my family and the next generation.

> *"They will still yield fruit in old age; They shall be full of sap and very green."*
> —Psalm 92:14

The Family of God

Producing and presenting radio programs is a unique experience, especially when the programs declare the gospel of Jesus Christ and teach the Word of God. I can't deny that I get discouraged sometimes though, since I live so far away from the listeners who hear programs that are pre-recorded sometimes thirty days in advance. I often wonder if people are truly listening and if the messages are having a positive impact. *Is it worth it for me to continue*, I ask myself? The encouraging response for me always comes from the Bible, where God says "So is my word that goes out from my mouth: It will not return to me empty but will accomplish what I desire and achieve the purpose for which I sent it" Isaiah 55:11. I read that and know I must have faith and believe that the messages, preached with sincerity of spirit, will produce fruit at the right time. My responsibility is to proclaim the whole counsel of God and allow the Holy Spirit to use the messages to change the hearts of the listeners and prepare them for eternity.

Another source of encouragement for me comes from the privilege that Helena and I have of traveling to the countries that air our programs. These trips are made possible by the generous financial support of friends who are also servants of God. During our travels, we have the opportunity to speak at different churches and have personal contact with the listeners, and it's this contact that enables us to gauge the impact of the Word that we sow into their lives. We also get to see up close the challenges and needs of the people and receive constructive feedback and suggestions on how to improve the programs as well as topics that need to be addressed in future messages.

While traveling within the country, we visit churches in various cities, villages, and remote areas. We are exposed to the different cultures and traditions of a diverse people living in the same nation. This requires a great deal of time, discernment, and patience from us. Yet contact with the people is often a highlight for us in this ministry, as it serves as a jolt of inspiration to continue moving forward. The time and money spent on these trips are well worth the investment because they not only help our listeners but us as well, as producers and messengers.

It's hard to describe the reaction of the listeners when they meet us for the first time. Some can't speak and simply shake their heads then they give us an inviting smile and a hug. Others just stand there and only start talking once we ask them what the programs means to them. We in turn get overwhelmed with emotions when they tell us what God has done in their lives. Pastors also share their gratitude for the programs and what they are doing for their churches as they bring in many new converts. Their words of gratitude are always followed by a request for us to be steadfast and continue in this good work.

> "Welcome him in the Lord with great joy, and honor men like him . . . ."
> —Philippians 2:29 (BSB)

My Age

I am well aware that there's coming a time, in the very near future, when I won't be able to produce and record messages any longer, and that's life. God gives us all a limited amount of time to serve while we have health and physical and mental strength. The aging process affects people in different ways. In my case, I noticed that my mental and physical agility are decreasing gradually. Tasks, like reading and producing programs, now take me double the time. In the studio I sometimes make technical errors while operating the equipment, which would never happen before. There have been times when during a recording session, I will press the wrong button unknowingly and disrupt the whole process, resulting in me spending time trying to figure out where I went wrong. Even my speech and tone of my voice is not the same. Essentially, these are all signs from God letting me know that my time to relinquish the microphone is near.

The question this raises is will the ministry end when these recordings cease? I don't believe so. We have received many suggestions, from several individuals in different countries, on what we should do. Sometimes I am reluctant to look for a replacement because on two previous occasions that required me to do so, the individuals did a subpar job, from mine and others' expectations. The ministries ended up suffering a great deal under my replacements' leadership. But I am encouraged to pass the baton to younger individuals that have been chosen by God.

The Ministry's Future: 2020 and Beyond
Yeva Ondaka

With the Trans World Radio Angola branch going bankrupt, the Igreja Evangelica Sudoeste de Angola (IESA) churches have decided to take over the production and financing of airtime for this program, which was under TWR Angola's administration. This transition began in 2019, in partnership with TWR Africa. As of right now, Angola produces six of the weekly programs, and I produce the seventh. With the IESA's help, I will look for someone who I can train and later give all the responsibilities of producing and recording my Saturday slot. *Yeva Ondaka* will also go through some restructuring, not in the content of the messages but in format and presentation. This program has been on the air for many years thanks to the financial support and prayers of the Swiss Alliance Mission, and the IESA church.

Character First

After eight years on the air in four countries, I am now looking for someone to take over the *Character First* program. Someone who has the same vision that motivated me to start it in the first place. It's not easy to find a person willing to take on this task because it is volunteer work that requires a lot of scientific and theological research. The whole concept of volunteering is not readily accepted in Africa because the poverty that plagues the continent makes it difficult for people to work without expecting some type of compensation. I've been praying that, at the right time, God will show me the right person and provide the financial support needed, just like He faithfully provided for me for over forty years. Until then, I've been selecting and re-editing messages from my archive of four hundred programs, choosing those that are not occasion sensitive and can be aired at any time. There is enough to cover a period of two to three years, and the plan is to make them available for re-air in the future. I'm also looking for individuals or churches that would be willing to cover the costs of airing the program in Portuguese-speaking countries. This financial support would also include an amount for a monthly donation for my replacement. My goal is to transfer these responsibilities by the end of 2020 when the program will celebrate its tenth anniversary.

> *"So he departed from there and found Elisha the son of Shaphat, while he was plowing with twelve pairs of oxen before him, and he with the twelfth. And Elijah passed over to him and threw his mantle on him."*
>
> —1 Kings 19:19

Conclusion

Time has been kind to me. It has given me the gift of being able to look back and see clearly the hand of God in my life and the purpose of each step over the years. As I start slowing down and time seems to speed up, I find that my focus and desire continues to be steadfast. The words in Psalms 67 describe it best:

1 May God be gracious to us and bless us and make his face shine on us.
2 so that your ways may be known on earth, your salvation among all nations.
3 May the peoples praise you, God; may all the peoples praise you.
4 May the nations be glad and sing for joy, for you rule the peoples with equity
 and guide the nations of the earth.
5 May the peoples praise you, God; may all the peoples praise you.
6 The land yields its harvest; God, our God, blesses us.
7 May God bless us still, so that all the ends of the earth will fear him.

May the radio ministry, and other instruments of communication, continue to be a strong tool for the churches in Angola and other countries. May they persevere in the task of reaching those who have not been reached with the gospel, so that Jesus Christ may be made known. May all the people of the earth praise the name of the Lord, the Creator and Sustainer of the universe. This has been my life's work and continual prayer.

Isac Silvano
Atlanta, Georgia
January 2020

Acknowledgments

Writing this book was a challenge for me. I am not a writer and had no intentions of writing a book or documenting my life's story. It was only after being prompted by several friends and acquaintances that I finally decided to put "pen to paper" and start this writing process. I look back now and realize how rewarding the experience was for me. I am grateful for God's help in enabling me to do this and to everyone who encouraged me to start and complete this project.

I would especially like to thank David Nutter whose counsel, support, and partnership was instrumental in bringing this to print.

I also want to thank my daughter Priscila, who helped me with the outline and several aspects of the writing process.

Finally, thank you to the publishing professionals at BookLogix for your hard work and turning this vision into a reality.

About the Author

Isac Silvano has been in full-time ministry and radio broadcasting for over forty years. He has pastored churches in Brazil, served as a missionary in Africa, and is now "retired" but continues to produce and record two radio programs, one of which began in 1976. His voice can be heard in various Portuguese speaking nations where his programs are aired. He and his wife and partner in ministry, Helena, call Atlanta, Georgia home.